# Robbery

"*An inclusive and informative review of robbery from varied perspectives that will provide a valuable insight to practitioners and scholars.*"
—Dr. Peter Hall, *Senior Lecturer in Forensic Investigations, Coventry University and former Detective Superintendent, Major Investigation Department, Staffordshire Police*

"*Robbery is an often-forgotten crime type that has a significant impact on individual victims and society more generally, but there is surprising little research on this topic. This book is, therefore, long overdue and fills an important gap in the literature. What's great about this book is its comprehensive coverage of the subject; from distal motivational factors through to the minutiae of crime scene behaviour and the dynamics of an individual offence, as well as issues relevant to investigation, policing and prevention. As such, this book is valuable to a range of practitioners, researchers and students.*"
—Dr. Matthew Tonkin, *Associate Professor in Criminology, University of Leicester and co-editor of* "Property crime: Criminological and psychological perspectives"

"Amy Burrell's book, exploring key characteristics and themes of robbery, provides comprehensive and authoritative insight into a previously little understood crime and contemporary criminal justice issue. Summarising central debates, key lines of enquiry and significant research in the area, the book provides a thorough and comprehensive overview of what we know about robbery; the crime, who commits it, who is affected by it, and how it might be addressed. New and exciting reconceptualisations of robbery are offered, capturing global insights and covering a range of perspectives. Innovative insights into policing and preventing robbery, including consideration of linking and profiling methods that can support operational activities, showcase a range of practical applications of empirical findings in the area, facilitating a more evidence-based approach to tackling robbery. With its focus on providing a more holistic understanding of robbery – including explorations of themes of both violent and acquisitive criminal behaviour, as well as the relevance of group dynamics in delineating patterns of offending - this book should constitute essential reading for any student of forensic psychology, policing, criminology, or criminal justice. It will also prove an indispensable reference for researchers, as well as an invaluable resource for professionals – especially those working within the criminal justice

domains - in helping understand how policy and practice should be tailored to better meet the needs and challenges of dealing with this unique offence."
—Dr. Laura Hammond, *Reader in Forensic Psychology and Director of the Crime and Society Research Centre, Birmingham City University, UK*

Amy Burrell

# Robbery

The Tipping Point Between Theft and Violence

Amy Burrell
School of Psychology
University of Birmingham
Edgbaston, UK

ISBN 978-3-030-93172-8     ISBN 978-3-030-93173-5  (eBook)
https://doi.org/10.1007/978-3-030-93173-5

© The Editor(s) (if applicable) and The Author(s), under exclusive license to Springer Nature Switzerland AG 2022
This work is subject to copyright. All rights are solely and exclusively licensed by the Publisher, whether the whole or part of the material is concerned, specifically the rights of translation, reprinting, reuse of illustrations, recitation, broadcasting, reproduction on microfilms or in any other physical way, and transmission or information storage and retrieval, electronic adaptation, computer software, or by similar or dissimilar methodology now known or hereafter developed.
The use of general descriptive names, registered names, trademarks, service marks, etc. in this publication does not imply, even in the absence of a specific statement, that such names are exempt from the relevant protective laws and regulations and therefore free for general use.
The publisher, the authors and the editors are safe to assume that the advice and information in this book are believed to be true and accurate at the date of publication. Neither the publisher nor the authors or the editors give a warranty, expressed or implied, with respect to the material contained herein or for any errors or omissions that may have been made. The publisher remains neutral with regard to jurisdictional claims in published maps and institutional affiliations.

Cover credit: © Melisa Hasan

This Palgrave Macmillan imprint is published by the registered company Springer Nature Switzerland AG
The registered company address is: Gewerbestrasse 11, 6330 Cham, Switzerland

*For Tom*

# Preface

It may be useful to provide a little background as to how this book has come about. At the start of my career, I was very fortunate to work as an academic researcher based in a police station. This early experience really helped me to understand the importance of drawing on practitioner experience when conducting research and I learned so many unexpected things just by being in this environment (learning by osmosis as I call it!). Many of the crime types we worked on were property offences (e.g. burglary, car theft, criminal damage) and I developed an interest in working on the, often forgotten or less publicised, day-to-day offences that impact on the public. When I started putting ideas together for my PhD, I asked my Chief Superintendent which crime type would be useful to investigate. He immediately said personal robbery as this is a high impact offence that comes around routinely as an issue. However, when I started researching/reading up in the area, I was surprised by how few books there were on this topic. I found a number of resources on commercial robbery (e.g. bank jobs, cash-in transit) but less on personal robbery than I was expecting. This book has primarily come about because I want to write the book I would have found useful during my PhD. However, there are other reasons too. In particular, as I work on robbery, it is impossible to ignore group dynamics. There has been a wealth of literature published on this, including research specifically relating to robbery, and I felt it would be useful to pull this together into a chapter within a book. I also feel that property crime should gain more attention from researchers. There is a lot of emphasis on sexual offending (completely understandably), but I think we are missing a trick by not doing more around property offences. Not only are these often high prevalence (and so actions to tackle them can really reduce crime statistics) but they are also very impactful on victims. For that reason, I feel more work should be done and, if this book inspires anyone to research robbery, then I will be happy.

This book draws heavily on the findings of my PhD and associated research. However, a key aim is to bring together knowledge of personal robbery from across the crime literature—e.g. from criminology, psychology, youth justice, gangs, group dynamics, etc.—to provide a more comprehensive resource on this crime type. I have therefore expanded the scope substantially beyond the PhD and updated with contemporary literature on robbery and associated topics. The book is UK focused but will bring in international literature where relevant. I hope I have managed to achieve this and readers will find the book useful.

Edgbaston, UK  
March 2022

Dr. Amy Burrell

**Acknowledgements** There are many people who made my PhD, and therefore this book, possible. In particular, I would like to thank colleagues from West Midlands Police and Northamptonshire Police who supported me in more ways than I can say here from extracting data to proof reading chapters. A special mention to Gary Herrington and John Bond who—amongst many other things—braved co-authoring papers with me. I would also like to thank my supervisors—Ray Bull and Clive Hollin—for their guidance and expertise.

# Contents

| | | |
|---|---|---|
| 1 | What Is Robbery and Why Is It Important? | 1 |
| 2 | Offenders and Motivations | 21 |
| 3 | Offence Behaviours and Methods | 37 |
| 4 | Group Dynamics | 51 |
| 5 | Behavioural Crime Linkage | 69 |
| 6 | Profiling Robbery Offenders | 97 |
| 7 | Policing and Prevention | 117 |
| 8 | Conclusion | 141 |
| Index | | 147 |

# About the Author

**Dr. Amy Burrell** has been researching in crime and policing for over 15 years. She graduated from University of Durham with a degree in Applied Psychology in 2002 before going onto complete an M.Sc. in Forensic Behavioural Science at University of Liverpool the following year. After 4 years working as a Research Fellow for the Jill Dando Institute of Crime Science, she returned to education to complete a PhD (part-time) in Forensic Psychology at the University of Leicester. Her PhD was on behavioural crime linkage (i.e. a method for identifying whether you can identify series of offences committed by the same person based on their crime scene actions) in personal robbery. After completing her PhD in 2013, Amy moved to the University of Birmingham to become the Network Facilitator for the Crime Linkage International Network (C-LINK) (www.crimelinkage.org). She then moved to teaching roles for 6 years—Lecturer in Forensic Psychology at Birmingham City University and Lecturer/Assistant Professor in Forensic Psychology at Coventry University—before returning to research in January 2021. She continues to guest lecture alongside her research role.

Amy's research interests include property crime—in particular, personal robbery, behavioural crime linkage, group offending, group decision-making, and violent crime.

# List of Figures

| | | |
|---|---|---|
| Fig. 1.1 | Robbery over time | 7 |
| Fig. 2.1 | Proportion of offences committed by Groups | 24 |
| Fig. 3.1 | Relationship between offender and victim | 39 |
| Fig. 6.1 | Routine Activity Theory | 106 |
| Fig. 7.1 | Rational Choice Theory—risks outweigh rewards | 120 |
| Fig. 7.2 | Problem Analysis Crime Triangle | 121 |
| Fig. 7.3 | Using the Crime Triangle to understand robbery | 121 |

# List of Tables

| | | |
|---|---|---|
| Table 1.1 | Economic and social costs of crime—personal robbery | 12 |
| Table 2.1 | Offending group size (% of total offences) | 24 |
| Table 3.1 | Approach methods (Burrell, 2012) | 41 |
| Table 5.1 | Checklist of behaviours | 75 |
| Table 5.2 | Median scores for behaviours | 78 |
| Table 5.3 | Predictive accuracy of regression models | 79 |
| Table 5.4 | Discrimination accuracy (linked versus unlinked1 samples) | 79 |
| Table 5.5 | Predictive accuracy of regression models controlling for area | 83 |
| Table 5.6 | Discrimination accuracy (linked versus unlinked1 and linked versus unlinked2 analyses) | 84 |
| Table 5.7 | Predictive accuracy (adding more variables) | 86 |
| Table 5.8 | Discrimination accuracy (adding more variables) | 87 |
| Table 5.9 | Frequency of GG, LL, and GL pairs | 87 |
| Table 5.10 | Discrimination accuracy for GG, LL, and GL pairs | 89 |

CHAPTER 1

# What Is Robbery and Why Is It Important?

**Abstract** The chapter will explain how robbery represents an overlap between theft and violence. There can be a lot of confusion about what robbery is (e.g. how this is different from snatch theft or burglary). Therefore, this chapter will outline what personal robbery is (e.g. legal definition) and is what it is not (e.g. we burgle houses and rob people). The difference between commercial versus personal robbery is provided for context. There will also be some discussion of how robbery is recorded. Recent statistics and other data relating to the prevalence of robbery and trends are included. The impact of robbery on victims (e.g. psychological, emotional, physical) and society is also explored. This chapter sets the context for the book.

**Keywords** Personal robbery · Theft · Burglary · Victimisation

### INTRODUCTION

This book argues that robbery represents a tipping point between theft and violence. There are elements of both within the offence and, what might start as a theft, can easily escalate to robbery. This chapter explains what robbery is providing an overview of robbery and related offences for

© The Author(s), under exclusive license to Springer Nature
Switzerland AG 2022
A. Burrell, *Robbery*,
https://doi.org/10.1007/978-3-030-93173-5_1

context. Hopefully, this will assist the reader to understand why robbery should always be framed from the perspective of both theft and violence.

## What is Robbery?

This book is about personal robbery. There are a lot of misconceptions about robbery including definitions, and so this chapter seeks to explain what personal robbery is (and is not!) and provide an overview of key characteristics and trends.

### *A Problem of Definition*

A key challenge for this book is drawing together relevant literature on personal robbery from across disciplines and timescales. The first challenge is that definitions can vary—for example, across countries; robbery is classified as a violent crime in the UK and USA but a property crime in India (Ashmore-Hills & Burrell, 2020). How the police record offences might also vary—for example, some countries (e.g. the UK) only record the most serious offence that occurs within a single incident, others record the offence which was the primary motive (e.g. New Zealand), and others report all offences committed during the incident (e.g. South Africa) (Ashmore-Hills & Burrell, 2020). This is important as it could mean the nature of robbery is quite different if comparing international samples—for example, if a rape included a robbery, this would appear in recorded crime data for robbery in some countries but not others. This might also mean some analyses are not possible (or data would need to be extracted differently) to examine particular subtypes of offences (such as sexual robbery—see Reale et al., 2021a, 2021b for research on this topic based on French data). Such differences are one reason for keeping this book focused to the UK (as far as possible).

The definition of personal robbery is quite clear if using a legal definition and focusing on one country (e.g. the UK) (more on this later). However, life is not that straightforward when looking at human behaviour and how we conceptualise and talk about crime. Therefore, researching this book necessitated wide-reaching explorations of the literature to try to capture and assimilate the most relevant findings.

A particular challenge has been raised by how robbery is presented in the academic literature. Sometimes definitions are not clear—this book focuses on personal offences (i.e. crimes that happen to individuals) rather than commercial offences (e.g. committed against businesses), and sometimes it has not been clear if the findings are applicable to personal offences or not. Some studies use more colloquial language referring to personal robbery as "mugging"—language that is emotive and has led some authors to discuss the resulting "moral panic" as the criminal justice system and politicians reacted to the issue. For example, Hall et al.'s seminal 1978 text "Policing the Crisis: Mugging, the State, and Law and Order" argues the term "mugging" is harmful and sensationalist and masks the deeper causes of robbery. The term "mugging" is still used however (e.g. Flatley, 2017). In addition, sometimes personal robbery is grouped in with other offences (e.g. as part of a definition of "street crime") and it can be difficult to unpick the particular findings that relate to this offence. There are also papers where robbery is used as the comparator but the focus is on another offence. Again, this means picking out the relevant findings from within a paper with a non-robbery focus. Even when using official statistics, it is not always possible to distinguish between commercial and personal robbery (Chow & Mawby, 2020).

## *Legislative Definition and Crime Recording*

This book will use the UK legal definition for personal robbery. To set the context for this, it is first important to explain what theft is. Theft is defined as "dishonestly appropriating property belonging to another with the intention of permanently depriving the other of it" (Theft Act, 1968). All of the elements have to be present for the offence to be considered a theft. Specifically, the offender:

- Dishonestly—e.g. uses deception to facilitate the offence
- Appropriate—i.e. takes or removes the item(s)
- Property—this can include physical property (e.g. bank card) and intangible property (the money in that bank account)
- Belonging to another—the property must belong to another at the time of appropriation
- With the intention of permanently depriving them of it—this is the key as the offender could claim they borrowed an item and planned to return it

In the United Kingdom…

"a person is guilty of robbery if he steals, and immediately before or at the time of doing so, and in order to do so, he uses force on any person or puts or seeks to put any person in fear of being then and there subjected to force".
(Theft Act, 1968)

In this offence, "steals" is interpreted in accordance with the definition of theft as outlined above (Crown Prosecution Service, 2019). The use or threat of force can include different types of crime behaviour—for example, if someone is assaulted (e.g. in response to resistance). It would not include instances where force is applied to the property rather than the person (e.g. pulling a bag cleanly off the victim's shoulder) (Home Office, 2021b) but would include situations where "a victim is under any impression from the offender's words or actions that the offender may use force" (Home Office, 2021b: 4). Thus, robbery is theft from a person but with the added element of threat or use of force. This is why robbery has been conceptualised as the tipping point between theft and violence in this book.

There are two types of robbery; personal and business (Home Office, 2021b). For business robbery, the Home Office counting rules specify that one crime is recorded for each business property targeted (Home Office, 2021b). Other offences might also be recorded depending on the circumstances—for example, if a robber kills someone during the offence, a homicide will also be recorded or if customers are robbed for personal property during the business robbery, these incidents would be counted as personal robberies (one per victim). However, other injuries may not be counted as separate offences—for example, if three employees are wounded during the offence, just the robbery would be counted. Personal robbery is counted as one offence per victim—for example, if two women are robbed during the same incident, this would be recorded as two robberies as there are two victims. The number of offenders is immaterial (unless there is evidence they are acting independently of each other) (Home Office, 2021b). A key component of the definition of robbery is the threat or use of force. This is what separates it from offences such as Theft from Person and Burglary. For example, burglary is committed against properties (Home Office, 2021a). If an offender uses force to steal from a person whilst committing a burglary, that offence becomes a robbery (Home Office, 2021b). It can be difficult to distinguish between robbery and theft from person—for example, if minimal force is used (Flatley, 2017). Although force or threat of force can be hard to determine, the counting rules (Home Office, 2021b) provide examples to help police make clear distinctions. For example, a pickpocketing offence would be theft from person, as would a snatch theft where the grab is not sufficient to pull the victim off balance. If the victim is unbalanced or knocked over the theft from person is upgraded to robbery (Home Office, 2021b). Thus, the way robbery is recorded is a very clear example of how robbery is the tipping point between theft and violence.

### *Personal versus Business Robbery*

Personal robberies are more common than business robberies (Chaplin et al., 2011; Flatley, 2017) making up the majority of overall robbery cases-90% between April 2019 and March 2020 (Office for National Statistics [ONS], 2021a). The legal definition of robbery is the same across both offence types (Theft Act, 1968) (just with different targets), and there are common features—for example, both typically involve groups (Smith, 2003) and intend to accomplish some form of material gain (Wüllenweber & Burrell, 2020). However, in reality these offences can look quite different. For example, personal robbery is more strongly associated with the use of physical force whereas business robberies are more likely to involve the use of firearms (McCluskey, 2013). Monetary gains may be higher in business robbery (Wüllenweber & Burrell, 2020), although there is evidence that substantial sums can be gained from personal robbery as well. For example, interviewees (robbers who targeted drug dealers) in work by Jacobs (2000) in the USA reported making thousands of dollars from individual offences (in drugs and/or cash). Victim resistance is typically higher in personal robberies (Alison et al., 2000) which could explain why injuries are more common in personal robbery (O'Brien & Burrell, 2020).

Given the differences between the offences, these are typically researched separately (Burrell, 2012) and Matthews (2002) argues that research that does not differentiate between the two categories should be interpreted with caution. Thus, this book focuses on personal robbery only. For the interested reader, there is a wealth of useful literature on business robbery covering a range of topics (from methods to prevention) and stretching back over 30 plus years. See, for example, Austin

(1988), Fichera et al. (2014), Hansen et al. (2014), Hornsby and Hobbs (2020), Hunter (1991), van Koppen and Jansen (1998), and Matthews (2002).

### Characteristics of Personal Robbery

As mentioned earlier, personal robbery is the theft of goods from an individual via threat and/or use of violence (Home Office, 2021b). It is typically committed by men against other men (Rennison & Melde, 2014), co-offending is common (Burrell, 2012; Smith, 2003; van Wilsem, 2009), and the majority of offenders are a stranger to the victim (86% in the year ending March 2020; ONS, 2020). Personal robbery is typically committed in public place (Rennison & Melde, 2014) but can cluster in certain types of places including the night-time economy (Haberman et al., 2013) and tourist attractions (Drawve et al., 2020). Violence is a key component of robbery and can be verbal or physical (Burrell, 2012). Weapons are used/displayed in approximately one-third of offences (Flatley et al., 2010), in particular knives (Barker et al., 1993; Flatley et al., 2010). Offenders often travel to the crime scene on foot but there have been increasing reports of offenders using other methods—for example, mopeds/motorbikes (Brown et al., 2019). For more information on offenders and motivations, see Chapter 2 and Chapter 3 for more on victims and methods. See Chapter 4 for a discussion of co-offending and group dynamics.

## WHY IS PERSONAL ROBBERY IMPORTANT?

There are many reasons why personal robbery is important. Although not as prevalent as other offences, robbery accounts for thousands of offences per year. It is also heavily concentrated in particular places, at particular times, and around particular people. Most importantly, its impact on victims—and society as a whole—should not be underestimated. These issues are all discussed in this section.

### Prevalence

The Crime Survey for England and Wales (CSEW) finds personal robbery typically accounts for around 1–3% of crime per year (Flatley, 2017). It also accounts for around 2% of police recorded crime (Flatley, 2017).

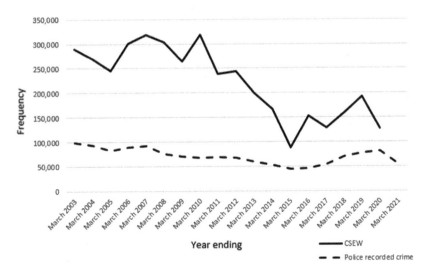

**Fig. 1.1** Robbery over time

Figure 1.1 shows the level of personal robbery over time as reported by the Crime Survey for England and Wales (CSEW) and Police Recorded Crime (generated using data from ONS, 2021a).

Rates were falling (after peaks in the 1980s and 1990s) (Flatley, 2017) with approximately 45–55,000 personal robberies per year between April 2013 and March 2017 (ONS, 2021a). However, the number of offences started to increase again peaking at 81,293 in the April 2019 to March 2020 period (ONS, 2021a). There was a substantial reduction (34%) in the year April 2020 to March 2021 (ONS, 2021a) but this accounted for by the COVID-19 pandemic when lockdown restrictions and the closure of the night-time economy led to people spending more time at home (Office for National Statistics, 2021b). Given the scale of offending, it is not surprising this offence type warrants some priority for the police.

*Concentration*

The majority of crime is usually attributable to a minority of places, situations, times, and people (Clarke & Eck, 2003; Pakkanen et al., 2012). Often this is reflected by a '80-20 divide' with approximately 20% of people/situations/places, etc., responsible for around 80% of crime.

Robbery, like all crime, clusters in time and space (Chow & Mawby, 2020; Monk et al., 2010; Tilley et al., 2004). For example, robbery is more concentrated in urban areas: in 2009/10, 62% of all robberies in England and Wales were recorded by just three (out of the 43) police forces. These forces—Metropolitan Police, Greater Manchester Police, and West Midlands Police—cover just 24% of the population (Flatley et al., 2010). In fact, the 80-20 rule applies, with further analysis of this data revealing that 20% of police forces accounted for 78% of robberies. The disproportionate clustering of offences is a trend that has been stable over time with these three police forces still accounting for around 60% of recorded robberies in work by Flatley (2017). This pattern is reflected in other countries as well with research from the Netherlands indicating robbery clusters at street level with 3% of streets accounting for 48% of street robberies and 75% of streets recording no robbery at all (van Wilsem, 2009).

On a more local level, personal robbery tends to cluster in locations where there are high volumes of people, such as night-time economy venues (Tilley et al., 2004), shopping areas, and other places where people gather. Transport hubs, in particular, are popular with robbers (Block & Davis, 1996; Gaziarifoglu et al., 2012) so much so that adding new stops to a bus route can increase robbery (Liu et al., 2020). Moreover, robbery is concentrated on particular bus routes (Loukaitou-Sideris, 1999), and at a small number of railway stations (Burrell, 2007; Walsh, 1999). Commercial robberies also cluster by location with research indicating that the same companies (Overall & Day, 2008), and even individual branches/stores (Matthews et al., 2001), are repeatedly targeted.

Robbery also clusters around people both in terms of victims and offenders. Repeat victimisation is well-documented in criminology literature (e.g. Farrell & Pease, 1993), and so it is unsurprising that 14% of robbery victims interviewed by the British Crime Survey in 2009/10 had been victimised more than once (Flatley et al., 2010). In fact, a recent rapid review identified repeat victimisation as common in robbery (Scottish Government, 2019). Vulnerable groups—for example, elderly people, young people/schoolchildren, and students (Smith, 2003; Tilley et al., 2004)—are popular targets for robbers. In terms of offenders, as mentioned above, the majority of offences are attributable to a minority of offenders (Clarke & Eck, 2003; Tilley & Laycock, 2002); commonly referred to as 'prolific' offenders. Prolific offenders present a significant challenge for criminal justice agencies and there is a national effort to target the offending committed by these individuals (e.g. the National Prolific and other Priority Offenders strategy and programme).

Robbery tends to be more frequent in the winter months (Landau & Fridman, 1993). This has been attributed to a range of factors including increased hours of darkness (van Koppen & Jansen, 1998), and weather conditions (i.e. colder weather means fewer people venture out thus making those who do more vulnerable to victimisation (Landau & Fridman, 1993)). Peak times for robbery are evenings and weekends (Cohn & Rotton, 2000; Monk et al., 2010; Smith, 2003). There are some exceptions which are often associated with the availability of prospective victims (Monk et al., 2010); for example, robberies involving schoolchildren commonly occur between 3 and 4 pm when they are travelling home from school and commuters using public transport are typically targeted during the evening rush hour (Tilley et al., 2004). Similarly, robberies of older people will cluster around the times they are likely to run errands (Monk et al., 2010) and evidence does show that robberies of people aged 65 and over tend to cluster in the mornings and early afternoon (in the USA; Klaus, 2000). Tilley et al. (2004) report elderly women are vulnerable to robbery in the daytime finding that offenders can take opportunities to target this group as they go about their daily routines.

## *Impact on Victims and Society*

The impact of personal robbery on victims can be wide-ranging including financial losses (e.g. due to the theft of goods), physical injury, and psychological harm. Financial loss is the most obvious impact of property crime (O'Brien & Burrell, 2020). For example, Heeks et al. (2018) report that the direct financial loss from stolen or damaged property was £1,030 for robbery. For context, this compares to £1,400 for domestic burglary and just £180 for theft from person.

Physical impacts of violent crime (including personal robbery) are that victims are more likely to sustain injuries, seek medical attention, and have physical health issues following the offence (Shapland & Hall, 2007; Tan & Haining, 2016). Research on prevalence of injuries varies. Some UK studies report injury rates of around 40% (e.g. Burrell, 2012; Smith, 2003) whereas others report lower rates (e.g. Barker et al., 1993, found that 28% of victims in over 5,500 street robberies were injured). Official statistics also report varying rates. For example, the Office for National Statistics (2020) report lower rates in some years (e.g. 25%

in 2016/2017 and 20% in 2019/2020) but higher in others (e.g. 41% in 2015/2016, 39% in 2017/2018, and 44% in 2018/2019). Types of injuries resulting from robbery include bruises, cuts, broken bones, and concussion (Heeks et al., 2018; ONS, 2020), and most are reported as minor. For example, the ONS (2020) report just 5% of injuries in 2019/2020 required medical attention and Barker et al. (1993) report 3% of injuries were serious in their sample. Burrell (2012) also found most injuries in her sample (88%; $n = 135$) were described as "slight". The remaining six (12%) were described as "serious" and were all committed by groups (indicating a potential extra threat from group offences). In Smith's (2003) work, the level of injury appeared to be directly related to the type of robbery, with most injuries being sustained in blitz attacks (where the initial contact with the victim is violence) compared to where snatching occurred (where the property is taken from the victim without any initial interaction at all). Victimisation can also result in indirect physical health issues (O'Brien & Burrell, 2020). For example, Gale and Coupe (2005) found many victims of robbery report somatic symptoms and insomnia three weeks post-offence, indicating the impact can be long-lasting.

The vast majority of victim's report being emotionally affected by the offence (89% in 2019/2020; ONS, 2020). Fear is common (ONS, 2020; Shapland & Hall, 2007) especially in street-based incidents where the offence happens in the context of the victim's everyday activities (Monk et al., 2010). Feelings can also include anger and shock (ONS, 2020; Shapland & Hall, 2007) as well as annoyance (54% in 2019/2020; ONS, 2020) and/or loss of confidence or feeling vulnerable (33% in 2019/2020; ONS, 2020). Mental health issues such as depression (ONS, 2020; Tan & Haining, 2016), panic attacks (ONS, 2020; Tan & Haining, 2016), and Post Traumatic Stress Disorder (PTSD) (Elklit, 2002; Gale & Coupe, 2005) can also occur. Furthermore, psychological harms—such as fear, depression, and anxiety—are likely to affect the victim for longer following a violent crime (Heeks et al., 2018). For example, Barker et al. (1993)—who conducted interviews with robbery victims—found that many reported long-lasting effects, with one reporting still being affected 18 months post-incident. Gale and Coupe (2005) also report long-lasting effects with trauma scores with an increase for one in five victims of personal robbery over time. In some cases, the fear and anxiety caused by robbery can lead to victims changing their behaviour. For example, they might stop wearing jewellery in an attempt to look like a less attractive target (Gale & Coupe, 2005) or avoid going out when it is dark (Tan & Haining, 2016).

The discussion so far has concentrated on the costs and impacts of robbery on the individual victim. However, the impacts of robbery are more wide-reaching. For example, as far back as 1978, Hall et al. talked about society reacts to robbery and (when framed as "mugging") that this can become a moral panic. Robbery has financial impacts for society as well. Heeks et al. (2018) found that, although the direct cost of robbery is £1,030, the overall estimated cost of a personal robbery is £11,320. This is because Heeks et al. (2018) take more than direct financial losses into account in their calculations. They also consider anticipated costs of crime and the cost of the response. Estimating the cost of crime is a complex endeavour and Heeks et al. (2018) provide a detailed explanation of how they have calculated their estimates which is useful to understand the broader impact of robbery. In their calculations, they considered the anticipated costs of crime, consequences, and cost of response. Their estimates, plus calculations from an earlier Home Office report on the economic and social costs of crime (Brand & Price, 2000), are summarised in Table 1.1.

These findings indicate that costs of crime are increasing in every area (e.g. anticipated costs, consequences, and response) and Heeks et al.'s (2018) estimate is more than double that calculated by Brand and Price's (2000). Even though the estimated number of offences is substantially lower in Heeks et al.'s (2018) work, the overall cost to society remains high at over £2 billion per annum. Other research also places a high price on robbery—for example, Lawson et al. (2018) calculated a robbery cost £9,796 (2015 prices).

Another way to estimate the impact of robbery (or any other crime for that matter) on society is to calculate harm or severity indexes. Sherman et al. (2016) argue this is more useful than counting and comparing frequencies of different offences as it takes into account the harm caused by crime. One of the best-known harm indexes is the Cambridge Harm Index (CHI). The CHI calculates harm scores for each offence type based on sentencing guidelines (Cambridge Centre for Evidence Based Policing, 2020). CHI scores are calculated by converting the minimum prison sentence for the offence into the number of days in prison. For example, for robbery (street and less sophisticated commercial) the starting point for a custodial sentence is one year and so the CHI is 365 (i.e. 1

**Table 1.1** Economic and social costs of crime—personal robbery

| Type of cost | Cost | Brand and Price (2000) | Heeks et al. (2018) |
|---|---|---|---|
| Anticipated cost | Defensive expenditure | £0 | £190 |
| | Insurance | £40 | £140 |
| Consequence | Property being stolen or damaged | £310 | £1,030 |
| | Physical and emotional harm | £2,400 | £3,590 |
| | Lost output (days off work/unproductive) | £420 | £920 |
| | Health services | £190 | £760 |
| | Victim services | £6 | £10 |
| Response | Police investigation | £1,400 (combined cost) | £1,010 |
| | Associated criminal justice system costs (jury, prosecution, court, legal aid, etc.) | | £3,670 |
| Total | | £4,700 | £11,320 |
| Estimated number of offences | | 420,000 | 193,470 |
| Estimated cost to society per annum | | £2 billion | £2.2 billion |

× 365 days) (Cambridge Centre for Evidence Based Policing, 2020). There are limitations to this approach—for example, using the minimum sentence assumes the crime is committed by a previously unconvicted offender and there are no aggravating factors (Sherman et al., 2016). To provide context, it is useful to consider what kind of offence would attract the starting point of 1 year in custody. This sentence would indicate a category C level of harm (no/minimal physical or psychological harm) from a situation which indicated lesser culpability (e.g. the offender was involved via coercion or exploitation, threat/use of force was minimal, and/or mental or learning disability linked to the commission of the offence) (Sentencing Council, 2021) which is not reflective of the range of robbery characteristics that might occur (e.g. use of a weapon would increase culpability (Sentencing Council, 2021)). Furthermore, Clark (2021) reports that the average sentence for robbery in 2020/2021 was 51.6 months—which is over 4 years and so substantially higher than this index scores this offence. However, Sherman et al. (2016) argue that, although the minimum custodial sentence does not precisely reflect offending, it is a more consistent metric than the alternative—i.e.

maximum sentence—which would be more distorting as it would only reflect the most serious offending. It is also reported that sentencing for robbery fluctuates over time (Ministry of Justice, 2020) and so, unless re-evaluating scores routinely, using average sentences to calculate CHI could be difficult to implement reliably.

A benefit of CHI is that it can be used to estimate an overall measure of harm for a particular crime type and/or in a particular area. For example, by multiplying the number of offences with the CHI score for that offence. Sherman et al. (2016) report 74,688 robberies multiplied by the CHI of 365 gives an overall number of prison days as 27,261,120. This can then be more appropriately compared to high occurring, lower harm offences (such as theft from vehicle (300,377 offences × 2 sentence days = 600,574) or lower occurring, higher harm offences (such as homicide (533 offences × 5,475 sentence days = 3,027,675)) which Sherman et al. (2016) argue provides a more meaningful measure of harm.

The Office for National Statistics have also developed a Crime Severity scoring system. This also uses sentencing outcomes to weight the harms for each offence type. In this instance, this is calculated using a formula which incorporates the proportion of offences which result in particular outcomes (custody, community order, fines) and average sentences or equivalencies (e.g. for fines the equivalency would be the amount of time it would take to earn the money to pay off the fine). Usefully, this metric has been developed into a practical data tool which can be used to calculate Crime Severity scores and rates of offences per 100,000 population for individual community partnership, police force, or region (Stripe, 2021). This tool provides weights for each offence type. For personal robbery, the weight is 800. However, the resource strongly indicates that weights for individual offence types cannot be directly compared (Stripe, 2021) and so weightings for other offences are not cited here for that reason. The tool is useful though to compare trends over time and across regions. Selecting Robbery for England, for example, indicates that the Crime Severity score has fluctuated over time starting at 1.7 (for the April 2002–March 2003 period) but falling consistently over time to 0.7 (the two years from April 2014 to March 2016) before increasing again raising to 1.2 for the April 2019–March 2020 period. Rates of robbery offences per 100,000 population have remained at 1 to 2 consistently over the same time period. The difference between severity score could be explained by differences in sentencing policy. Sherman et al. (2016) suggested that CHI scores could be averaged over 5 years to increase reliability as small fluctuations in high-tariff offences such as robbery can result in large effects on harm estimates. It is suggested the same effect might occur here given the Crime Severity score is also based on sentencing outcomes. For example, there was a 17% reduction in the proportion of robbery offenders sentenced to immediate custody in the 5 years up to March 2020 (Ministry of Justice, 2020). However, further examination revealed that sentences to immediate custody had increased by 5% in the most recent portion of that period (1-year period ending March 2020) (Ministry of Justice, 2020) indicating how sentencing can fluctuate over time. There are some consistent trends though—in particular, although the proportion of robbery offenders receiving an immediate custodial sentence might change year on year (Ministry of Justice, 2019), this group has consistently had the largest proportion of immediate custody outcomes for the period 2008 to 2018 (Ministry of Justice, 2019).

## Conclusion

To summarise, robbery represents a serious offence which impacts on individual victims and society as a whole. As such, it warrants attention from researchers to broaden our understanding of the offence. This book will go on to discuss different aspects of personal robbery—as identified by research to date—with a view to drawing together key knowledge to date. The focus is on the UK but international research will be cited as appropriate.

## References

Alison, L., Rockett, W., Deprez, S., & Watts, S. (2000). Bandits, cowboys and Robin's men: The facets of armed robbery. In D. Canter & L. Alison (Eds.), *Profiling property crimes* (pp. 75–106). Ashgate Publishing.

Ashmore-Hills, L., & Burrell, A. (2020). What is property crime? In A. Burrell & M. Tonkin (Eds.), *Property crime: Criminological and psychological perspectives* (pp. 9–21). Routledge.

Austin, C. (1988). *The prevention of robbery in building society branches. Crime Prevention Unit paper 14.* Home Office.

Barker, M., Geraghty, J., Webb, B., & Key, T. (1993). *The prevention of street robbery* (Police research group crime prevention unit series paper no. 44). Home Office. http://rds.homeoffice.gov.uk/rds/prgpdfs/fcpu44.pdf

Block, R., & Davis, S. (1996). The environs of rapid transit stations: a focus for street crime or just another risky place. In R. Clarke (Ed.), *Preventing mass transit crime. Crime Prevention Studies volume 6* (pp. 238–257). Criminal Justice Press.

Brand, S., & Price, R. (2000). *The economic and social costs of crime* (Home Office Research Study 217). Home Office.

Brown, I., Thompson, A., Pepper, I., & Ryan, M. (2019). *Mobile-enabled mobile phone snatches: A tale from two London boroughs*. European Law Enforcement Research Bulletin Nr. 18 (Winter).

Burrell, A. (2007). *Violence on and around public transport*. UCL Jill Dando Institute of Crime Science.

Burrell, A. (2012). *Behavioural case linkage in personal robbery* (PhD thesis). University of Leicester. https://leicester.figshare.com/articles/thesis/Behavioural_Case_Linkage_in_Personal_Robbery/10147652/1

Cambridge Centre of Evidence-Based Policing. (2020). *The Cambridge Crime Harm Index 2020 Update*. https://www.cambridge-ebp.co.uk/the-chi

Chaplin, R., Flatley, J., & Smith, K. (2011). *Crime in England and Wales 2010/11*. Home Office. https://www.gov.uk/government/uploads/system/uploads/attachment_data/file/116417/hosb1011.pdf

Chow, L., & Mawby, R. I. (2020). CCTV and robbery in high-rise public housing in Hong Kong. *Safer Communities, 19*(3), 119–130. https://doi.org/10.1108/SC-03-2020-0012

Clark, D. (2021). *Average length of prison sentences for offences in England and Wales 2020*. https://www.statista.com/statistics/1100192/prison-sentence-length-in-england-and-wales-by-offence/

Clarke, R. V., & Eck, J. (2003). *How to become a problem solving crime analyst*. Jill Dando Institute of Crime Science.

Cohn, E. G., & Rotton, J. (2000). Weather, seasonal trends, and property crimes in Minneapolis 1987–1988. A moderator-variable time- series analysis of routine activities. *Journal of Environmental Psychology, 20*, 257–272. https://doi.org/10.1006/jevp.1999.0157

Crown Prosecution Service. (2019). *Theft Act Offences*. https://www.cps.gov.uk/legal-guidance/theft-act-offences

Drawve, G., Caplan, J., Kennedy, L. W., & Sarkos, J. (2020). Risk of robbery in a tourist destination: A monthly examination of Atlantic City, New Jersey. *Journal of Place Management and Development, 13*(4), 429–446. https://doi.org/10.1108/JPMD-07-2019-0064

Elklit, A. (2002). Acute stress disorder in victims of robbery and victims of assault. *Journal of Interpersonal Violence, 17*, 872–887. https://doi.org/10.1177/0886260502017008005

Farrell, G., & Pease, K. (1993). *Once bitten, twice bitten: repeat victimisation and its implications for crime prevention* (Police Research Group Crime Prevention Unit Series Paper 46). Home Office.
Fichera, G. P., Fattori, A., Neri, L., Musti, M., Coggiola, M., & Costa, G. (2014). Posttraumatic stress disorder among bank employee victims of robbery. *Occupational Medicine, 65,* 283–289. https://doi.org/10.1093/occmed/kqu180
Flatley, J. (2017). *Overview of robbery and theft from the person: England and Wales.* Office for National Statistics. https://www.ons.gov.uk/peoplepopulationandcommunity/crimeandjustice/articles/overviewofrobberyandtheftfromtheperson/2017-07-20
Flatley, J., Kershaw, C., Smith, K., Chaplain, R., & Moon, D. (2010). *Crime in England and Wales 2009/10. Findings from the British Crime Survey and police recorded crime* (2nd ed.). Home Office Statistical Bulletin 12/10. Home Office. http://rds.homeoffice.gov.uk/rds/pdfs10/hosb1210.pdf
Gale, J., & Coupe, T. (2005). The behavioural, emotional and psychological effects of street robbery on victims. *International Review of Victimology, 12,* 1–22. https://doi.org/10.1177/026975800501200101
Gaziarifoglu, Y., Kennedy, L. W., & Caplan, J. M. (2012). *Robbery risk as a co-function of space and time.* Rutgers Center on Public Security.
Hall, S., Critcher, C., Jefferson, T., Clarke, J., & Roberts, B. (1978). *Policing the crisis: Mugging, the state, and law and order.* Palgrave Macmillan.
Haberman, C. P., Groff, E. R., & Taylor, R. B. (2013). The variable impacts of public housing community proximity on nearby street robberies. *Journal of Research in Crime and Delinquency, 50*(2), 163–188.
Hansen, M., Armour, C., Shevlin, M., & Elklit, A. (2014). Investigating the psychological impact of bank robbery: A cohort study. *Journal of Anxiety Disorders, 28,* 454–459. https://doi.org/10.1016/j.janxdis.2014.04.005
Heeks, M., Reed, S., Tafsiri, M., & Prince, S. (2018). *The economic and social costs of crime* (Home Office Research Report 99). Home Office.
Home Office. (2021a). *Home Office Counting Rules for Recorded Crime: Burglary.* https://assets.publishing.service.gov.uk/government/uploads/system/uploads/attachment_data/file/977205/count-burglary-apr-2021.pdf
Home Office. (2021b). *Home Office Counting Rules for Recorded Crime: Robbery.* https://assets.publishing.service.gov.uk/government/uploads/system/uploads/attachment_data/file/977204/count-robbery-apr-2021.pdf
Hornsby, R., & Hobbs, D. (2020). Armed robbery (commercial). In *Oxford research encyclopedias: Criminology and criminal justice.* https://doi.org/10.1093/acrefore/9780190264079.013.392
Hunter, R. (1991). Environmental crime prevention: An analysis of convenience store robberies. *Security Journal, 2*(2), 78–82.

Jacobs, B. A. (2000). *Robbing drug dealers: Violence beyond the law*. Walter de Gruyter Inc.

Klaus, P. (2000). *Crimes Against Persons Age 65 or Older, 1992– 1997. No. NCJ 176352*. Bureau of Justice Statistics, Office of Justice Programs.

Landau, S. F., & Fridman, D. (1993). The seasonality of violent crime: The case of robbery and homicide in Israel. *Journal of Research in Crime and Delinquency, 30*, 163–191.

Lawson, T., Rogerson, R., & Barnacle, M. (2018). A comparison between the cost effectiveness of CCTV and improved street lighting as a means of crime reduction. *Computers, Environment and Urban Systems, 68*, 17–25. https://doi.org/10.1016/j.compenvurbsys.2017.09.008

Liu, L., Lan, M., Eck, J., & Lei King, E. (2020). Assessing the effects of bus stop relocation on street robbery. *Computers, Environment and Urban Systems, 80*, 101455. https://doi.org/10.1016/j.compenvurbsys.2019.101455

Loukaitou-Sideris, A. (1999). Hot spots of bus stop crime. The importance of environmental attributes. *Journal of the American Planning Association, 65*, 395–411.

Matthews, R. (2002). *Armed robbery*. Routledge.

Matthews, R., Pease, C., & Pease, K. (2001). Repeated bank robbery: Theme and variations. In G. Farrell & K. Pease (Eds.), *Crime prevention studies* (Vol. 12, pp. 153–164). Criminal Justice Press.

McCluskey, J. D. (2013). A comparison of robbers' use of physical coercion in commercial and street robberies. *Crime & Delinquency, 59*(3), 419–442. https://doi.org/10.1177/0011128709352233

Ministry of Justice. (2019). *Criminal Justice Statistics Quarterly, England and Wales, Year Ending December 2018*. https://assets.publishing.service.gov.uk/government/uploads/system/uploads/attachment_data/file/802032/criminal-justice-statistics-quarterly-december-2018.pdf

Ministry of Justice. (2020). *Criminal Justice Statistics Quarterly, England and Wales, April 2019 to March 2020*. https://assets.publishing.service.gov.uk/government/uploads/system/uploads/attachment_data/file/910530/criminal-justice-statistics-quarterly-march-2020.pdf

Monk, K. M., Heinonen, J. A., & Eck, J. E. (2010). *Street robbery* (Problem-Oriented Guides for Police Problem-Specific Guides Series No. 59). https://cops.usdoj.gov/RIC/Publications/cops-p181-pub.pdf

O'Brien, F., & Burrell, A. (2020). The impact of property crime on victims. In A. Burrell & M. Tonkin (Eds.), *Property crime: Criminological and psychological perspectives* (pp. 59–74). Routledge.

Office for National Statistics. (2020). *Nature of Crime: Crime (data tables)*. https://www.ons.gov.uk/peoplepopulationandcommunity/crimeandjustice/datasets/natureofcrimerobbery

Office for National Statistics. (2021a, July). *Crime in England and Wales: Appendix Tables.* https://www.ons.gov.uk/peoplepopulationandcommunity/crimeandjustice/datasets/crimeinenglandandwalesappendixtables

Office for National Statistics. (2021b, July). *Crime in England and Wales: Year Ending March 2021.* https://www.ons.gov.uk/peoplepopulationandcommunity/crimeandjustice/bulletins/crimeinenglandandwales/yearendingmarch2021#types-of-violencehttps://www.birmingham.ac.uk/index.aspx

Overall, C., & Day, G. (2008). The Hammer Gang; an exercise in the spatial analysis of an armed robbery series using the probability grid method. In. S. Chainey & L. Tomson (Eds.) *Crime mapping case studies: Practice and research* (pp. 55–62). Wiley.

Pakkanen, T., Zappalà, A., Grönroos, C., & Santtila, P. (2012). The effects of coding bias on estimates of behavioural similarity in crime linking research in homicide. *Journal of Investigative Psychology and Offender Profiling, 9*(3), 223–234. https://doi.org/10.1002/jip.1366

Reale, K. S., Beauregard, E., & Chopin, J. (2021a). Comparing the crime-commission process involved in sexual burglary and sexual robbery. *Criminal Justice and Behavior.* Advance online publication. https://doi.org/10.1177/00938548211023541

Reale, K. S., Beauregard, E., & Chopin, J. (2021b). Expert versus novice: criminal expertise in sexual burglary and sexual robbery. *Sexual Abuse.* Advance online publication. https://doi.org/10.1177/10790632211024236

Rennison, C. M., & Melde, C. (2014). Gender and robbery: A national test. *Deviant Behavior, 35*(4), 275–296. https://doi.org/10.1080/01639625.2013.848104

Scottish Government. (2019). *Repeat violent victimisation: A rapid evidence review.* http://www.svru.co.uk/wp-content/uploads/2020/02/repeat-violent-victimisation-rapid-evidence-review.pdf

Sentencing Council. (2021). *Robbery—Street and less sophisticated commercial.* https://www.sentencingcouncil.org.uk/offences/crown-court/item/robbery-street-and-less-sophisticated-commercial/

Shapland, J., & Hall, M. (2007). What do we know about the effects of crime on victims? *International Review of Victimology, 14*, 175–217. https://doi.org/10.1177/026975800701400202

Sherman, L., Neyroud, P. W., & Neyroud, E. (2016). The Cambridge Crime Harm Index: Measuring total harm from crime based on sentencing guidelines. *Policing, 10*(3), 171–183. https://doi.org/10.1093/police/paw003

Smith, J. (2003). *The nature of personal robbery* (Home Office Research Study 254). Home Office. http://library.npia.police.uk/docs/hors254.pdf

Stripe, N. (2021). *Crime in England and Wales: Year Ending December 2020.* https://www.ons.gov.uk/peoplepopulationandcommunity/crimeandjustice/bulletins/crimeinenglandandwales/yearendingdecember2020

Tan, S., & Haining, R. (2016). Crime victimisation and the implications for individual health and well-being: A Sheffield case study. *Social Science & Medicine, 167*, 128–139. https://doi.org/10.1016/j.socscimed.2016.08.018

Theft Act 1968. https://www.legislation.gov.uk/ukpga/1968/60/contents

Tilley, N. & Laycock, G. (2002). *Working out what to do: Evidence-based crime reduction* (Crime Reduction Research Paper 11). Home Office.

Tilley, N., Smith, J., Finer, S., Erol, R., Charles, C., & Dobby, J. (2004). *Problem solving street crime: Practical lessons from the street crime initiative.* Home Office.

van Koppen, P., & Jansen, R. (1998). The road to robbery: Travel patterns in commercial robberies. *British Journal of Criminology, 38*(2), 230–246.

van Wilsem, J. (2009). Urban streets as micro contexts to commit violence. In D. L. Weisburd, W. Bernasco, & G. J. N. Bruinsma (Eds.), *Putting crime in its place: Units of analysis in geographic criminology* (pp. 199–216). Springer.

Walsh, B. (1999). *Safety on public transport: A project to explore the extent of victimisation and the main crime and safety issues for staff and passengers of the Adelaide transport system, South Australia.* National Crime Prevention and the Crime Prevention Unit, South Australia Attorney Generals Department.

Wüllenweber, S., & Burrell, A. (2020). Offence characteristics: A comparison of lone, duo, and 3+ perpetrator robbery offences. *Psychology, Crime, and Law.* https://doi.org/10.1080/1068316X.2020.1780589

CHAPTER 2

# Offenders and Motivations

**Abstract** This chapter will focus on who commits robbery and why. It will outline the different motivations for robbery (e.g. money, peer pressure, excitement, links with drug use/funding a habit). Gangs will also be discussed where relevant. The chapter will link to relevant academic theory (e.g. Developmental Taxonomy [Moffitt in *Psychological Review* 100:674–701, 1993], Social Learning Theories, Social Control Theories). The chapter will also touch on the growth of technology and personal possessions and how this has created opportunities for robbery.

**Keywords** Developmental Taxonomy · Social Control Theory · Social Learning Theory · Social Dynamics · Street Capital · Motivation

## INTRODUCTION

Explanations for why people commit robbery are varied. This chapter will first outline who commits personal robbery before moving on to discuss motivations for committing the offence and theoretical explanations for offending behaviour (in so far as these pertain to robbery).

## Who Commits Personal Robbery?

This section outlines the demographics of robbery offenders.

### *Gender*

The vast majority of robberies were committed by men (between 84 and 97% in the British Crime Survey each year; Flatley, 2017). This trend is found in other research as well—for example, 90% of offenders in Wüllenweber and Burrell (2020) were male. Burrell (2012) reports 93% of her sample ($n = 360$ total offenders) were recorded as male. Other research also reports the majority of suspects in street robberies are male (e.g. Monk et al., 2010; Smith, 2003).

### *Age*

Robbery offenders tend to be young (Monk et al., 2010). For example, Burrell (2012) reports age ranges of 10–45 with an average of 18–19 at the time of the offence in her samples. Wüllenweber and Burrell (2020) report a slightly higher age range (11–52 years) and average (22 years) though the most commonly age reported was 17. Other studies also report that the age profile of robbery offenders has increased over time. For example, Flatley (2017) reports that over half of offenders were aged 25 or over in the year ending March 2017 compared to one in five in the year ending March 2006. Sentencing data also shows this trend with fewer young people (aged under 21) convicted of robbery than in previous years (Ministry of Justice, 2016).

### *Ethnicity*

The relationship between ethnicity and robbery is complex and sourcing reliable statistics on the ethnic breakdown of offenders has proved difficult. The so-called associations between black youth and robbery are common but even early work on robbery critiques these links arguing that society represents a discriminatory environment (Hall et al., 1978), and it is argued robbery is subject to racial stereotypes (see, for example, O'Flaherty & Sethi, 2008), with a perception that robbery is disproportionately committed by Black individuals. This is reflected in the criminal justice system in the UK where ethnic minority individuals are over-represented as defendants (Yasin & Sturge, 2020) including robbery (Roberts & Bild, 2021), and research has found White offenders can be under-represented and Black people over-represented within samples. For example, Burrell (2012) reported that, in one sample, only 69% of offenders were White compared to a local population estimate of 91%. In another area, half of offenders in the sample were Black despite this ethnic group only making up 6% of the local population. Arrest statistics indicate Black individuals account for a disproportionately high level of robbery arrests both in the USA (Monk et al., 2010) and the UK (Bowling & Phillips, 2007; UK Parliament, 2007). Furthermore, Yasin and Sturge (2020) report offenders from ethnic minority backgrounds receive longer custodial sentences. It has also been demonstrated that Black individuals—especially young Black men—are disproportionately stopped and searched under the Police and Criminal Evidence Act (PACE) 1984 (Bowling & Phillips, 2007; Equality & Human Rights Commission, 2010). If powers are used disproportionately, it is not surprising that a higher proportion of offenders from a particular ethnic group might be identified. All of these complexities make it difficult to unpick the relationship between ethnicity and robbery (if there is one).

### *Groups*

Personal robberies are commonly committed by groups (Smith, 2003). The Crime Survey for England and Wales (CSEW) (ONS, 2020) reported that between 42 and 71% of robberies were committed by groups between 2009/2010 and 2019/2020 (see Fig. 2.1).

Group sizes can vary—for example, two (duos), three (trios), or groups or 4 or more (ONS, 2020). Table 2.1 shows the proportion of offences committed by each group size for a 5-year period based on data from CSEW (ONS, 2020). It is clear that the most common group size each year tends to be duos, however, the distribution can vary from year to year.

Robbery is a group offence but this does not mean it is always committed by organised gangs. Co-offending is common (van Wilsem, 2009) and sometimes the connection between co-offenders might be loosely structured friendship groups rather than organised crime groups (Harding et al., 2019). Having said this, gang members do commit robberies though the nature of these offences might vary depending on the group (e.g. young street gangs will commit opportunistic offences

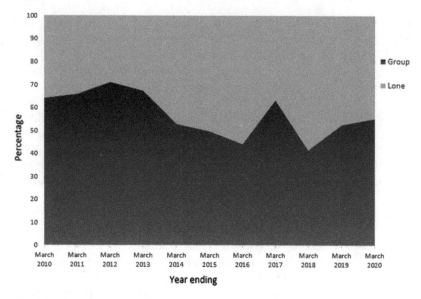

**Fig. 2.1** Proportion of offences committed by Groups

**Table 2.1** Offending group size (% of total offences)

| Year ending | Group size (% of robberies) | | | |
| --- | --- | --- | --- | --- |
| | Lone | Duo | Trio | Four or more offenders |
| March 2016 | 56 | 19 | 14 | 11 |
| March 2017 | 37 | 33 | 6 | 25 |
| March 2018 | 58 | 22 | 7 | 12 |
| March 2019 | 48 | 28 | 13 | 12 |
| March 2020 | 45 | 19 | 13 | 23 |

whereas more organised crime gangs are more specialised and commit more complex offences [Harding et al., 2019]).

## WHY DO THEY COMMIT PERSONAL ROBBERY?

There are lots of reasons why people might commit robbery. This section will outline some of the key motivations offenders report for committing robbery. It also outlines some theoretical explanations for offending that could be applied to robbery.

## *Motivations*

### *Money*

The most obvious reason to commit robbery is for material gain and some offenders (e.g. serious and organised crime groups) will pay particular attention to maximizing profits (Harding et al., 2019). Most often, this will be cash but items which can be quickly exchanged for cash (or used as currency) such as jewellery and drugs are also popular targets. There is a lot of evidence that the desire for money acts as driver for property crime (Tonkin, 2020) with many researchers reporting this as a common motivation (e.g. Alarid et al., 2009; Monk et al., 2010; Muniz & Powers, 2021). The reasons offenders report needing money varies. Whilst some report needing to commit robbery to overcome financial hardship (e.g. Whittaker et al., 2020), this does not appear to be a key driver (Tonkin, 2020). More often, research finds that offenders are using their ill-gotten gains to fund a party lifestyle and/or buy luxury items such as cars, designer clothes, and jewellery (e.g. Brookman et al., 2007; Jacobs & Wright, 1999; Jacobs et al., 2003; Shover & Honaker, 1992). Money can be such a key motivator that, if it becomes less profitable (or other things become more profitable), it could result in a reduction in robbery offences (Whittaker et al., 2020).

### *Substance Misuse*

Substance misuse—e.g. drug and/or alcohol use or addiction—is strongly associated with acquisitive crime. Robbery can occur if the offender is trying to fund a habit (Alison et al., 2000; Tilley et al., 2004) or this could be related to a loss of impulse control associated with substance use. Whatever the reason, substance misuse is a key driver for robbery. An independent review of drug use in the UK by Dame Carol Black (2020) estimated that nearly half of acquisitive crimes (excluding fraud) are drug-related. Breaking this down by offence type, the review estimated that over a quarter (27.6%) of personal robberies were drug-related (Black, 2020). It has been reported that robbers can be motivated to offend to fund a drug habit (Tilley et al., 2004). Furthermore, evidence from the Crime Survey for England and Wales reports that victims perceive offenders to be under the influence of drugs in 17% to 30% of personal robberies each year. Lower levels are reported for perception that the offender is under the influence of alcohol but this still represented between 9 and 27% of personal robberies per year (year ending March 2010 to year ending March 2020) (ONS, 2020).

*Impressing Your Peers*
Property crime is a means to enhance an offender's status within their social group (Tonkin, 2020) and research has found that street robbery is associated with the desire to appear tough in front of peers (Barker et al., 1993). For example, Harding (2014) found young street gangs see robbery as a means to gain peer approval or build "street capital". Furthermore—following on from the last point about money—committing robbery provides the funds to maintain a lifestyle that might be used to impress peers (Monk et al., 2010). Although the peer influence tends to diminish over time, it is argued to be the most important causal factor for crime between the ages of 12–18 (Tonkin, 2020). Given that robbery offenders tend to be young, peer influence is considered a key motivator for this kind of offending.

*Thrill*
It has been reported that offenders commit robbery to alleviate boredom (Tilley et al., 2004), as "playful maneuvers" (Katz, 1991), or for the "buzz" (Alarid et al., 2009; Brookman et al., 2007; Deakin et al., 2007; Young et al., 2007). Excitement is a particular motivation for young street gangs (as opposed to more organised criminal groups), also giving them the opportunity to "bond" with peers (Harding et al., 2019).

*Revenge*
Research interviewing robbers about their offending have repeatedly found references to revenge. For example, Brookman and colleagues (2007) report a number of examples of revenge robberies including a female offender who robbed a male in retaliation for him sexually assaulting her friend. Robbery might also be used as a form of debt collection, with offenders reporting they would use robbery as a way to recoup money they were owed (Wright et al., 2006). Robbery can also be used in revenge for being robbed themselves (Jacobs, 2000). Thus, for offenders (a group of people who might not want to risk reporting incidents to the police [Tonkin, 2020]), robbery provides an opportunity for getting

justice (Jacobs, 2000). Robbery can also be used as a method of scaring rivals (Harding et al., 2019).

*Accident*
Some offenders report that they committed robbery by accident (Jacobs, 2000). This typically occurs when the offender is in the midst of something else (e.g. socialising or committing a different crime) and the situation escalates into a robbery.

*Opportunity*
It has been posited that offenders can be in a state of "alert opportunism" (Bennett & Wright, 1984) which refers to a willingness to offend if the right opportunity comes up (Jacobs et al., 2003). Personal robbery is often impulsive (Jacobs, 2000) and offenders will take opportunities to commit robberies if they see them. For example, seeing someone withdraw large amounts of cash from an ATM alone and/or intoxicated (Monk et al., 2010).

Opportunity can also arise from social changes and technological advances. In terms of social changes, the average value of goods that we carry around with ourselves has increased markedly (e.g. it is not unusual for a person to be carrying a phone, a laptop, and/or other devices on their person as these have become more portable). This makes robbery more profitable and so could lead to increases in robbery rates. Changing social norms can also increase opportunities for robbery. For example, mask wearing became expected during national lockdowns in the UK during the COVID-19 pandemic. Masks increase anonymity, reducing the risk of being recognised, which can, in turn, increase the risk of street robbery (Sheard & Farrell, 2020). In contrast, social changes can also reduce opportunities for crime—for example, lockdown restrictions and the closure of the night-time economy was attributed to a fall in robbery during the COVID-19 pandemic (as people were spending more time at home) (Office for National Statistics, 2021). Technological advances can also create opportunities for crime. For example, the introduction of contactless card payments increases the potential rewards of crime including robbery (Farrell & Tilley, 2021a, 2021b).

## Theoretical Explanations

There are a number of theories from criminology and psychology that have been developed to try to explain offending behaviour. There are many theories of crime but some are more applicable to robbery than others. A few of the core theoretical ideas are summarised below with explanations for how these might apply to personal robbery.

### Developmental Taxonomy

Robbery is largely committed by younger offenders (Monk et al., 2010). With this in mind, it is worth considering what might explain why young people commit more offences. One of the most prominent theories in this area is Moffitt's (1993) Developmental Taxonomy. This theory proposes that there are two distinct pathways to crime—(1) the Life Course Persistent Offender (LCP) and (2) the Adolescent Limited Offender (AL). LCP offenders commit crime across their life course whereas AL offenders demonstrate an increase in offending between the ages of 12 and 17 with a sharp drop off after this point. Moffitt (1993) suggests that LCP offenders have genetic risk factors (e.g. that could expose them to brain abnormalities) that could predispose them to commit crime. Combined with environmental factors—such as poor upbringing, parental-child conflict, and difficult social circumstances—the LCP individual is more likely to follow a path that will lead to offending. For example, LCP individuals often lack the opportunities to develop prosocial skills or disengage with education (Moffitt, 1993; Souverein et al., 2016). It is therefore not surprising that they might turn to crime (including robbery) to make money (Tonkin, 2020) and so this may explain why older individuals can become embedded in a life of crime.

However, research consistently shows most offenders fall into the AL pathway (e.g. Loeber & Farrington, 2014; Moffitt, 1993). Crime is disproportionately committed by young people (Kelly, 2011) and Moffitt (1993) accounts for this through the AL pathway. She posits that AL offenders experience a maturity gap whereby teenagers are unable to legitimately access the same benefits as adults (e.g. buying alcohol, driving, buying a house, etc.). During this time, individuals might turn to offending to earn money to buy what they want. However, as soon as the teenager is able to purchase those goods legitimately or take that life step (e.g. get married), they turn away from offending. This explains why they only offend for a short period during adolescence. There are clear parallels to motivations described above—for example, the desire for money and wanting to impress peers—which could be explained well by the Developmental Taxonomy.

*Social Control*
Social Control approaches propose that crime happens as a result of a weakened or broken bond with society (Casey, 2011). The argument is that if someone does not feel part of society, they do not feel the obligation to adhere to societal rules (Tonkin, 2020). Research has demonstrated that property crime offenders can have weak societal links—for example, through the identification of "street culture" (see, for example, Shover & Honaker, 1992; Wright et al., 2006; Wright & Decker, 1994). A commitment to a party lifestyle rather than more traditional values can be associated with offending (e.g. to earn enough to fund their lifestyle) (Tonkin, 2020), and social control theory can be applied to robbery (Hirshi, 1986).

*Social Learning*
Social Learning Theory (SLT) (Bandura, 1971, 1973) argues that behaviour is learned from our observations of, and interactions with, other people. In the famous Bobo doll experiment (Bandura et al., 1961), children witnessed an adult hitting a doll and later mimicked that behaviour and so was developed into a theory to explain aggressive behaviour. Social learning approaches have been used to explain the propensity to commit crime (Tonkin, 2020) arguing that offenders develop pro-crime attitudes through observing others (Felson & Lane, 2009; Pratt et al., 2010).

Interactions with others also influence behaviour (Akers, 2001) as people will mimic the behaviour of others if they see them being rewarded for that behaviour (Akers, 2001). This mimicking of behaviour will be repeated if it is reinforced by rewards and/or reinforcement (Tonkin, 2020). Brauer (2009) demonstrated that friend and family reinforcement for theft could be used to predict theft behaviour (in a USA sample), and Wright and Decker (1994) reported burglars interviewed in their sample indicated they committed offences as a result of being prompted by friends. However, a meta-analysis conducted in 2010 suggested that SLT might not be operating quite as expected; instead of individuals being influenced to adopt their friends' pro-crime attitudes, it could be that association with criminal peers just offers access to more suitable targets (Pratt et al., 2010). Research (from the USA) has found an association between experiencing physical abuse and committing violent crime (including robbery) (Felson & Lane, 2009) indicating some influence of learning from social experiences on crime. Furthermore, research from Nigeria (Otu, 2010) has demonstrated that the way offenders commit robbery is influenced by who/what they learn from (e.g. robbers who learned through reading or watching screens (rather than from friends or family) were more likely to plan their offences, allocate roles, and use weapons).

*Social Dynamics*
Weaver and Fraser (2021) argue that theoretical explanations of group offending often fail to consider how social dynamics of relationships impact on offending decisions (including desistence). Rooted in sociology—especially the work of Bourdieu (2005) and Donati (2011)—the authors argue that individuals, and the networks between them, do not occur in isolation. These social relations are not just the influence of one person on another, but capture the more complex effects of mutual interactions (Donati, 2011). This can result in relational goods (e.g. loyalty, trust) but also relational harms (e.g. control, fear) (Donati, 2011). If individuals want to maintain relational goods, they might behave in ways they might not do otherwise (Weaver & Fraser, 2021). When considering the interaction of such a theory with the motivation to impress peers, this would explain why individuals who may not offend alone might become involved in group offending. Weaver and Fraser (2021) also discuss the importance of Bourdieu's (2005) work on habitus, i.e. socially ingrained habits, skills, and dispositions. It is argued that habitus is learned through socialisation rather than individual processes, and—once formed—the habits are transferred from one situation to another. In sum, Weaver and Fraser (2021) draw on core sociological theory to argue it is essential that social relations and habitus are considered when trying to understand and explain why people commit crime.

*Street Capital*
Weaver and Fraser (2021) are not the only researchers to draw on Bourdieu's work—Harding applies these principles in his work on gangs. He argues that, in the gang environment, success is determined by building and maintaining street capital and this is a tradable asset (Harding, 2012). Interviews with gang members—who commit violent crime including

robbery—found that younger members had less street capital but they were seeking to build this (McLean et al., 2018). Conversely, older members had street capital and were using this to exploit other members and make financial gains. Furthermore, personal robbery can be a strategic action taken by offenders to gain street capital as it can support youngsters to develop and hone their skills (Harding et al., 2019). Thus, street capital—and the desire to build this—is crucial to our understanding of why young people (e.g. in gangs) commit robbery.

There are a wealth of theories of crime and the summaries above are just that—summaries. They introduce some explanations but there is much more written on these in the literature for interested readers. Good reviews of theories of crime include DeLisi (2005) and Farrington and Tfoti (2017). For more discussion of Social Dynamics specifically, see Weaver and Fraser (2021).

## Conclusion

This chapter has outlined who is associated with committing robbery, in short, young males. The range of motivations are varied. Money is a key driver either directly or indirectly (e.g. to fund a party lifestyle and/or drug habit). However, some offenders have reported committing robbery for non-monetary reasons including to gain "street capital" and for excitement. There are a range of theoretical explanations for why people commit robbery. Some key theories—namely Developmental Taxonomy, Social Learning Theory, Social Control Theory, Social Dynamics Theory, and Street Capital—have been outlined with links made to their specific relevance to robbery.

## References

Akers, R. L. (2001). Social learning theory. In R. Paternoster & R. Bachman (Eds.), *Explaining criminals and crime: Essays in contemporary criminological theory* (pp. 192–210). Roxbury.

Alarid, L. F., Burton, V. S., & Hochstetler, A. L. (2009). Group and solo robberies: Do accomplices shape criminal form? *Journal of Criminal Justice, 37*, 1–9. https://doi.org/10.1016/j.jcrimjus.2008.12.001

Alison, L., Rockett, W., Deprez, S., & Watts, S. (2000). Bandits, cowboys and Robin's men: The facets of armed robbery. In D. Canter & L. Alison (Eds.), *Profiling property crimes* (pp. 75–106). Ashgate Publishing.

Bandura, A. (1971). *Social learning theory*. General Learning Press. http://www.asecib.ase.ro/mps/Bandura_SocialLearningTheory.pdf

Bandura, A. (1973). The social learning theory of aggression. In R. Falk & S. S. Kim (Eds.), (1980). *The war system: An interdisciplinary approach* (pp. 141–157). Routledge.

Bandura, A., Ross, D., & Ross, S. (1961). Transmission of aggression through imitation of aggressive models. *The Journal of Abnormal and Social Psychology, 63*(3), 575–582.

Barker, M., Geraghty, J., Webb, B., & Key, T. (1993). *The prevention of street robbery*. Police research group crime prevention unit series paper no. 44. Home Office. http://rds.homeoffice.gov.uk/rds/prgpdfs/fcpu44.pdf

Bennett, T. & Wright, R. (1984). *Burglars on burglary: Prevention and the offender*. Gower.

Black, C. (2020). *Review of drugs—Evidence relating to drug use, supply and effects, including current trends and future risks*. https://assets.publishing.service.gov.uk/government/uploads/system/uploads/attachment_data/file/882953/Review_of_Drugs_Evidence_Pack.pdf

Brauer, J. R. (2009). Testing social learning theory using reinforcement residue: A multilevel analysis of self-reported theft and marijuana use in the National Youth Survey. *Criminology, 47*(3), 929–970.

Bourdieu, P. (2005). Habitus. In J. Hillier & E. Rooksby (Eds.), *Habitus: A sense of place* (pp. 43–52). Ashgate.

Bowling, B., & Phillips, C. (2007). Disproportionate and discriminatory: Reviewing the evidence on police stop and search. *The Modern Law Review, 70*(6), 936–961. https://doi.org/10.1111/j.1468-2230.2007.00671.x

Brookman, F., Mullins, C., Bennett, T., & Wright, R. (2007). Gender, motivation and the accomplishment of street robbery in the United Kingdom. *British Journal of Criminology, 47*, 861–884. https://doi.org/10.1093/bjc/azm029

Burrell, A. (2012). *Behavioural case linkage in personal robbery* [PhD thesis, University of Leicester]. https://leicester.figshare.com/articles/thesis/Behavioural_Case_Linkage_in_Personal_Robbery/10147652/1

Casey, S. (2011). Understanding young offenders: Developmental criminology. *The Open Criminology Journal, 4*, 13–22.

Deakin, J., Smithson, H., Spencer, J., & Medina-Ariza, J. (2007). Taxing on the streets: Understanding the methods and process of street robbery. *Crime Prevention and Community Safety, 9*, 52–96. https://doi.org/10.1057/palgrave/cpps.8150033

DeLisi, M. (2005). Developmental theory and its application. In M. DeLisi (Ed.), *Career criminals in society* (pp. 51–76). Sage.

Donati, P. (2011). *Relational sociology: A new paradigm for the social sciences*. Routledge.

Equality and Human Rights Commission. (2010). *Stop and think: A critical review of the use of stop and search powers in England and Wales.* https://www.equalityhumanrights.com/sites/default/files/ehrc_stop_and_search_report.pdf

Farrell, G. & Tilley, N. (2021a). Contactless card payment limits and crime rates after the pandemic. UCL JDI Special Series on COVID-10: No. 26. https://www.ucl.ac.uk/jill-dando-institute/sites/jill-dando-institute/files/26_contactless_payments_final.pdf

Farrell, G., & Tilley, N. (2021b). *"Tap-and-PIN": Preventing crime and criminal careers from increased contactless payments.* UCL JDI Special Series on COVID-10: No. 28. https://www.ucl.ac.uk/jill-dando-institute/sites/jill_dando_institute/files/tap_and_pin_no_28.pdf

Farrington, D. P., & Tfoti, M. M. (2017). Developmental and psychological theories of offending. In G. M. Davies & A. R. Beech (Eds.), *Forensic psychology: Crime, justice, law, interventions* (3rd ed., pp. 73–92). Wiley-Blackwell.

Felson, R. B., & Lane, K. J. (2009). Social learning, sexual and physical abuse and adult crime. *Aggressive Behavior, 35,* 489–501.

Flatley, J. (2017). *Overview of robbery and theft from the person: England and Wales.* Office for National Statistics. https://www.ons.gov.uk/peoplepopulationandcommunity/crimeandjustice/articles/overviewofrobberyandtheftfromtheperson/2017-07-20

Hall, S., Critcher, C., Jefferson, T., Clarke, J., & Roberts, B. (1978). *Policing the crisis: Mugging, the state, and law and order.* Palgrave Macmillan.

Harding, S. (2012). *The role and significance of street capital in the social field of the violent youth gang in Lambeth* [PhD thesis, University of Bedfordshire].

Harding, S. (2014). *The Street Casino.* Policy Press.

Harding, S., Deuchar, R., Densley, J., & McLean, R. (2019). A typology of street robbery and gang organization: Insights from qualitative research in Scotland. *British Journal of Criminology, 59,* 879–897.

Hirshi, T. (1986). On the compatibility of rational choice and social control theories of crime. In D. B. Cornish & R. V. Clarke (Eds.), *The reasoning criminal: Rational choice perspectives on offending* (pp. 105–118). Springer-Verlag.

Jacobs, B. A. (2000). *Robbing drug dealers: Violence beyond the law.* Walter de Gruyter Inc.

Jacobs, B. A., Topalli, V., & Wright, R. (2003). Carjacking, streetlife and offender motivation. *British Journal of Criminology, 43,* 673–688.

Jacobs, B. A., & Wright, R. (1999). Stick-up, street culture, and offender motivation. *British Journal of Criminology, 37,* 149–173. https://doi.org/10.1111/j.1745-9125.1999.tb00482.x

Katz, J. (1991). The motivation of the persistent robber. *Crime and Justice, 14*, 277–306.

Kelly, R. (2011). *What makes juvenile offenders different from adult offenders?* Trends & issues in crime and criminal justice no. 409. Australian Institute of Criminology. https://www.aic.gov.au/publications/tandi/tandi409

Loeber, R., & Farrington, D. P. (2014). Age-crime curve. In D. Weisburd & G. Bruinsma (Eds.), *Encyclopedia of criminology and criminal justice* (pp. 12–18). Springer.

McLean, R., Deuchar, R., Harding, S., & Densley, J. (2018). Putting the 'street' in gang: Place and space in the organization of Scotland's drug-selling gangs. *British Journal of Criminology, 59*(2), 396–415. https://doi.org/10.1093/bjc/azy015

Ministry of Justice. (2016). *Criminal justice statistics quarterly, England and Wales, 2016 (final)*. https://assets.publishing.service.gov.uk/government/uploads/system/uploads/attachment_data/file/614414/criminal-justice-statistics-quarterly-december-2016.pdf

Moffitt, T. E. (1993). Adolescence-limited and life-course-persistent antisocial behavior: A developmental taxonomy. *Psychological Review, 100*, 674–701. https://doi.org/10.1037/0033-295X.100.4.674

Monk, K. M., Heinonen, J. A., & Eck, J. E. (2010). *Street Robbery. Problem-Oriented Guides for Police Problem-Specific Guides Series No. 59*. https://cops.usdoj.gov/RIC/Publications/cops-p181-pub.pdf

Muniz, C. N., & Powers, R. A. (2021). Applying the classic rape scenario to robbery: An examination of situational characteristics and reporting victimization to police. *Journal of Criminal Justice, 72*, 101737. https://doi.org/10.1016/j.jcrimjus.2020.101737

O'Flaherty, B., & Sethi, R. (2008). Racial stereotypes and robbery. *Journal of Economic Behavior & Organization, 68*(3–4), 511–524. https://doi.org/10.1016/j.jebo.2008.06.007

Office for National Statistics. (2020). *Nature of crime: Crime (data tables)*. https://www.ons.gov.uk/peoplepopulationandcommunity/crimeandjustice/datasets/natureofcrimerobbery

Office for National Statistics. (2021, July). *Crime in England and Wales: Year ending March 2021*. https://www.ons.gov.uk/peoplepopulationandcommunity/crimeandjustice/bulletins/crimeinenglandandwales/yearendingmarch2021#types-of-violencehttps://www.birmingham.ac.uk/index.aspx

Otu, S. E. (2010). Armed robbery and armed robbers in contemporary Nigeria: The social learning and model revisited. *International Journal of Criminology and Sociological Theory, 3*(2), 438–456.

Police and Criminal Evidence Act (PACE) 1984. https://www.legislation.gov.uk/ukpga/1984/60/part/I

Pratt, T. C., Cullen, F. T., Sellers, C. S., Winfree, T., Jr., Madensen, T. D., Daigle, L., Fearn, N. E., & Gau, J. M. (2010). The empirical status of social learning theory: A meta-analysis. *Justice Quarterly, 27*(6), 765–802. https://doi.org/10.1080/07418820903379610

Roberts. J. V., & Bild, J. (2021). *Ethnicity and custodial sentencing: A review of trends, 2009–2019.* https://sentencingacademy.org.uk/wp-content/uploads/2021/06/Ethnicity-and-Custodial-Sentencing-1.pdf

Sheard, E. & Farrell, G. (2020). *COVID facemasks as crime facilitators.* UCL JDI Special Series on COVID-10: No. 23. https://www.ucl.ac.uk/jill-dando-institute/sites/jill-dando-institute/files/covid_facemasks_as_crime_facilitators.pdf

Shover, N., & Honaker, D. (1992). The socially bounded decision making of persistent property offenders. *Howard Journal of Criminal Justice, 31,* 276–293. https://doi.org/10.1111/j.1468-2311.1992.tb00748.x

Smith, J. (2003). *The nature of personal robbery.* Home Office Research Study 254. Home Office. http://library.npia.police.uk/docs/hors254.pdf

Souverein, F. A., Ward, C. L., Visser, I., & Burton, P. (2016). Serious, violent young offenders in South Africa: Are they life-course persistent offenders? *Journal of Interpersonal Violence, 31*(10), 1859–1882. https://doi.org/10.1177/0886260515570748

Tilley, N., Smith, J., Finer, S., Erol, R., Charles, C., & Dobby, J. (2004). *Problem-solving street crime: Practical lessons from the Street Crime Initiative.* Home Office.

Tonkin, M. (2020). The pathway to property crime. In A. Burrell & M. Tonkin (Eds.), *Property Crime: Criminological and psychological perspectives* (pp. 23–38). Routledge.

UK Parliament. (2007, June). *Nature and extent of young Black people's over-representation.* https://publications.parliament.uk/pa/cm200607/cmselect/cmhaff/181/18105.htm

van Wilsem, J. (2009). Urban streets as micro contexts to commit violence. In D. L. Weisburd, W. Bernasco & G. J. N. Bruinsma (Eds.), *Putting crime in its place: Units of analysis in geographic criminology* (pp. 199–216). New York: Springer.

Weaver, B., & Fraser, A. (2021). The social dynamics of group offending. *Theoretical Criminology,* 1–21. https://doi.org/10.1177/13624806211030459

Whittaker, A., Densley, J., Cheston, L., Tyrell, T., Higgins, M., Felix-Baptiste, C., & Havard, T. (2020). Reluctant gangsters revisited: The evolution of gangs from postcodes to profits. *European Journal on Criminal Policy and Research, 26,* 1–22. https://doi.org/10.1007/s10610-019-09408-4

Wright, R. T., & Decker, H. (1994). *Burglars on the job: Streetlife and residential break-ins.* Northeastern University Press.

Wright, R., Brookman, F., & Bennett, T. (2006). The foreground dynamics of street robbery in Britain. *British Journal of Criminology, 46*, 1–16.

Wüllenweber, S., & Burrell, A. (2020). Offence characteristics: A comparison of lone, duo, and 3+ perpetrator robbery offences. *Psychology, Crime, and Law.* https://doi.org/10.1080/1068316X.2020.1780589

Yasin, B. & Sturge, G. (2020). *Ethnicity and the criminal justice system: what does recent data say on over-representation?* https://commonslibrary.parliament.uk/ethnicity-and-the-criminal-justice-system-what-does-recent-data-say/

Young, T., FitzGerald, M., Hallsworth, S., & Joseph, I. (2007). *Groups, gangs, and weapons.* Youth Justice Board. ISBN 978-1-906139-06-3.

CHAPTER 3

# Offence Behaviours and Methods

**Abstract** This chapter focuses on offence behaviours and methods of committing personal robbery. This includes target selection, types of approach used (e.g. blitz, con), property stolen, and weapon display and use. Offender adaptation and overlaps with other offences are considered—e.g. a car thief who now needs the key to steal a car might escalate to robbery to achieve the theft.

**Keywords** Robbery · Weapon use · Target selection · Offender adaptation

## INTRODUCTION

Personal robbery can be committed in a number of ways but there are common trends. This chapter outlines trends in personal robbery in the UK. This will include victim selection, approach, violence and control (including weapon use and co-offenders), and property stolen.

## VICTIM/TARGET SELECTION

The vast majority of victims of personal robbery are men. The Crime Survey for England and Wales (CSEW) reports a ratio of 71% male

© The Author(s), under exclusive license to Springer Nature Switzerland AG 2022
A. Burrell, *Robbery*,
https://doi.org/10.1007/978-3-030-93173-5_3

37

to 29% female (year ending March 2020; Office for National Statistics (ONS), 2020). This represents 90,000 offences against men and 37,000 offences against women each year (ONS, 2020). Other research mirrors this trend—for example, Wüllenweber and Burrell (2020) report 73% of victims were male compared to 26% female (gender of victim was unknown in 1% of cases). Burrell (2012) also reports most robbery victims are male (79–84%). There are a number of reasons why this might be the case. For example, interviews with robbers have identified a morality around target selection where women and children are avoided (author experience), and research by de Hann and Vos (2003) indicates street robbers adopt moral boundaries.

Although people of all ages are reported to be victims of robbery, most are young. For example, Burrell (2012) reports robbery victims were commonly teenagers and young adults. Wüllenweber and Burrell (2020) report victims' ages ranged from 6 to 88 years. However, the average age was 26 years and the most frequently recorded age was 19.

Victims can be of any ethnicity, but some groups appear to be at an increased risk. For example, Burrell (2012) reports 9% of victims in her sample were Black (West Midlands) despite only making up 6% of the population at time. Wüllenweber and Burrell (2020) also found some ethnic minority groups were over-represented as victims (e.g. Asian). Other groups were under-represented (e.g. White individuals). Black people are disproportionately victims of violent crime (Commission on Race & Ethnic Disparities, 2021). This includes robbery—for example, an inquiry by the Mayor of London (UK) found Black people were 1.6 times more likely to be victims of robbery (UK Parliament, 2007).

Offenders are typically strangers to the victim; it is perhaps easier (morally) to rob someone you do not know and/or there is less chance of retribution (Jacobs, 2000). The CSEW reports the proportion of offences committed by strangers as 86% in the year ending March 2020 (ONS, 2020). The remaining offences were committed by people known by sight or to speak to (13%) or known well (1%). These proportions vary from year to year but at least 70% are committed by strangers each year (April 2010–March 2020) (ONS, 2020) (see Fig. 3.1; generated based on data from ONS 2020).

However, it is important to note that victims may not always report robbery, even to the CSEW or if they know the offender. For example, if they fear repercussions from an acquaintance who robbed them (Felson et al., 2000) or the victim is an offender themselves (Jacobs, 2000). It

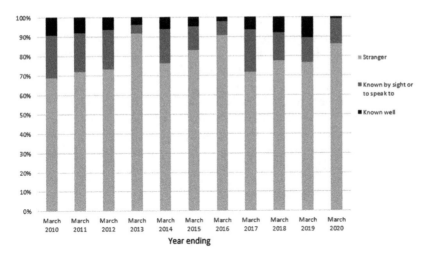

Fig. 3.1 Relationship between offender and victim

is further noted that the CSEW captures the experiences of people aged 16 and over (whilst data on 10–15-year olds has also been gathered since 2009, this forms a separate dataset and is not included in Fig. 3.1). This is important as it has been reported that the age of victims can vary widely and certainly includes young people. For example, Tilley et al. (2004) highlighted school children as a group vulnerable to street crime, including robbery. Furthermore, Felson et al. (2000) reported that a fifth of victims in their sample were aged under 18, and that this group was particularly vulnerable to robbery by known-by-sight-only and non-family acquaintances. Thus, it could be that the robbery data is not reflecting the true picture of what is happening, especially with regards to younger victims. Particular types of people are targeted by robbers. For example, tourists (Drawve et al., 2020; Monk et al., 2010), students (Monk et al., 2010), and drug dealers (Jacobs, 2000). Drug dealers, in particular, are a popular target. Dealers often carry lots of cash or drugs (Jacobs, 2000) and are not likely to report offences to the police (Jacobs, 2000; Tita & Greenbaum, 2009).

Burrell (2012) found robbery offenders do not tend to travel far to commit their offences. For example, the average was just 2,447 metres in one police force area (Northamptonshire) and 2,045 metres in the other (West Midlands). The shorter distance is perhaps unsurprising given West

Midlands is a considerably smaller police force geographically and more urbanised. Groups tend to travel further than lone offenders (Burrell, 2012); perhaps due to a greater awareness of good opportunities to commit crime or because the decision to commit robbery happens when already out doing something else.

Robbery is heavily concentrated in urban areas presumably due to an abundance of targets. Research (from the Netherlands) has found that the presence of transport hubs and adjacency to a high street are both positively associated with street robbery (van Wilsem, 2009); both busy places which present offenders with a range of targets. Furthermore, Flatley (2017) reports that around 60% of robberies are consistently recorded by just three police forces in England and Wales. These forces, namely the Metropolitan Police, West Midlands, and Greater Manchester all, despite being geographically small compared to other police force areas, contain large conurbations. In terms of types of locations, there is evidence that robbery clusters in particular kinds of places. The CSEW identified key locations for personal robbery in England and Wales as the street (29% of robberies in the year ending March 2020), around home (15%), around work (12%), near/on transport (6%), and around pubs/clubs (3%) (ONS, 2020). Similar types of locations are identified as hotspots for robbery in other countries too. For example, Caplan and colleagues (2020) found that bus stops were the most prevalent risk factor for street robbery in Jersey City, USA. In fact, bus stops are consistently found to be associated with robbery (e.g. Gerell, 2018; Hart & Miethe, 2014; Liu et al., 2020; Loukaitou-Sideris, 1999). Other types of locations positively associated with robbery include bars, restaurants, and off-licenses (Bernasco & Block, 2011); perhaps not surprising as alcohol-impaired customers might provide a target for robbers (Roncek & Maier, 1991). Cashpoints have also been associated with personal robbery (Burrell, 2012; Hart & Miethe, 2014; Wüllenweber & Burrell, 2020)— for example, Monk et al. (2010) report that offenders target young people using ATMs alone at night/when they are intoxicated.

## Approach

Once the decision is made to commit the robbery and the target chosen, the next step is to plan the approach. Robberies do not all take the same course of action (Wüllenweber & Burrell, 2020). There are differences in approach style (Goodwill et al., 2012). Smith (2003) classified approach into "blitz", "confrontation", "con", "snatch", and "victim initiated", and was able to allocate almost all offences (99.7%) into one of these categories. Burrell (2012) identified six approach methods (see Table 3.1).

However, Burrell (2012) was not always been able to categorise the approach for the offences in her sample. Specifically, she was only able to identify how the offender approached the victim in 39% of cases in Northamptonshire and 29% in the West Midlands. The problems identifying approach could be due to what data were available and/or how this information was coded. For example, when Burrell completed inter-rater reliability analysis, she and her rater colleague disagreed on approach the most often, in particular what constituted a "blitz" attack. This indicates that some behaviours are harder to code reliably than others (Burrell, 2012).

Regardless of issues with reliably coding approach method, it is clear a range of approaches are used. Distraction and con methods are common but other methods such as surprise or blitz might also be used (Burrell,

**Table 3.1** Approach methods (Burrell, 2012)

| Approach type | Definition |
| --- | --- |
| Dupe | The modus operandi suggested that dupe tactics were used to set up the robbery, e.g. a fake advert or posing as a delivery man |
| Carjacking | The victim was targeted for the car |
| Offender breaks into/forces entry into premises | The offender(s) broke into the victim's home including where the victim disturbs a break in or the offender forced their way into the property (e.g. kicking the door in) |
| Approach from behind | The offender(s) approach the victim from behind |
| Distraction | The modus operandi indicates that distraction was used to set up the robbery, e.g. do you have the time, do you have a light, do you have change, can you spare 20p |
| Blitz | The modus operandi indicates that the offence was a blitz attack, i.e. immediate violence was used |

2012). Many offenders arrive at the crime scene on foot but there have been increasing reports of offenders using mopeds/motorbikes (Brown et al., 2019) or pedal cycles to facilitate their offences. For example, in the 12 months up to February 2018, there were over 1,300 thefts/robberies in one London borough where a moped was used (Brown et al., 2019). Of course, the vehicle itself might be the target so the offender could arrive on foot but leave on stolen property (e.g. pedal cycle, moped, or car).

## Violence and Control

A key component of robbery is violence or the threat of violence (Home Office, 2021). Violence and control can take many forms in a personal robbery. For example, Luckenbill (1980) reported different means of executing force that include threats, prodding, or incapacitating. Burrell (2012) reported four methods of control offenders used during robbery that fall into these categories. Firstly, verbal threat (e.g. attempts to scare the victim, this does not include arguments). Secondly, violence—physical contact (e.g. grabbed, pushed, or restrained victim, blocking their escape), and violence—physical assault (e.g. holding a knife to the victim's throat). Finally, offender physically controls victim (i.e. forced the victim to go somewhere such as taking them to a cashpoint to withdraw money). The prevalence of controlling behaviours differed across the two police force areas in Burrell's (2012) study. In the rural area (Northamptonshire), verbal threats were more common (41% of offences) although a third of cases (32%) involved a physical assault. Physical contact was reported less frequently (23% of offences) and there were very few instances where the victim was forced somewhere (less than 3% of cases). In contrast, verbal threats were less common in the more urban environment (West Midlands) reported in just 28% of cases. Physical assault was also around a third of cases (35%) but physical contact was higher than in Northamptonshire (34%). Again, forcing the victim to go somewhere was rare, occurring in just over 5% of cases.

Burrell (2012) also identified a number of controlling behaviours used by offenders specifically to steal property, namely requesting property, demanding property, snatching/grabbing, and forcing a search upon the victim. The most common method was demanding (31% of crimes in both West Midlands and Northamptonshire). Offenders tended to demand that victims hand over property, although some did use more casual approaches—for example, asking to use their phone and then refusing to return the item. Searching was also a common method in West Midlands (31% of cases compared to 15% of cases in Northamptonshire) and this was often associated with group offences (Burrell, 2012).

*Weapon Use*

Weapon use is another indicator of violence. Estimates of weapon use vary—for example Flatley (2017) reports that between one fifth and one third of robberies include a weapon. Similar levels are reported by Burrell (2012) (37–41%) and Wüllenweber and Burrell (2020) who report weapons were present in 14–21% of offences and used in 23–38% of robberies in their sample. Where weapons are used, this is most commonly a knife (Barker et al., 1993; Burrell, 2012; Flatley, 2017; ONS, 2020) but recorded levels of knife use in offences can vary by area. For example, Burrell (2012) found a much higher proportion of offences were recorded as involving a knife in West Midlands (72%) than Northamptonshire (36%). This could reflect a difference between urban and rural environments or a difference in definitions or recording practices. It is also noted that the sample size was much smaller in Northamptonshire ($n = 59$) compared to West Midlands ($n = 228$) which could explain differences. Thus, although interesting to note a difference, more research would be needed to determine (1) if this was a real difference—i.e. if offenders in one area really do use knives less often, and (2) why this might be.

Other kinds of weapons include knuckledusters (Burrell, 2012), and coshes/batons/hitting implement (Burrell, 2012; ONS, 2020) although this depends how you define weapon as Wüllenweber and Burrell (2020) reported fists were used on 20–34% of offences in their sample. Firearms—a weapon which is commonly associated with robbery in other countries (such as the USA) are rarer in personal robberies in the UK (e.g. Burrell (2012) found only 2–3% of robberies in her sample included firearms). Similarly, the ONS (2020) reports firearms are only reported in between 0–4% of robberies each year (April 2009–March 2020). This is most likely due to stricter firearms regulations and restrictions which reduces access to such weapons (Crown Prosecution Service, 2017). Some offences involve multiple weapons—where this is the case, the offences are (unsurprisingly) committed by groups (Burrell, 2012) presumably with offenders having a weapon each. However, the presence of weapons are more commonly associated with lone offenders (Burrell, 2012; Burrell et al., 2015). This is not surprising as groups of offenders have different methods of control available to them. For example, strength in numbers (Porter & Alison, 2006b).

### *Violence by Groups*

A large majority of personal robberies are committed by groups (see Chapter 4 for more on group dynamics). This is relevant to methods as (as mentioned above) the group provides a means of controlling victims. Research on other violent crime—e.g. rape—has demonstrated that the number of offenders can influence the control strategies used (see da Silva et al., 2013; Lundrigan & Mueller-Johnson, 2013) and it is predicted this would be the same for robbery (Wüllenweber & Burrell, 2020). Some evidence of this has been found by Burrell et al. (2015) in their research on behavioural crime linkage. A core part of this work was testing the similarity of behaviours across two offences committed by the same offender. In cases where the offender was alone in one offence and part of a group in the other, differences in how the offences were committed became apparent, especially in relation to control (Burrell et al., 2015). These differences in behaviour could be influenced, not just by the group context, but (more specifically) the number of people in the group (Wüllenweber & Burrell, 2020). For example, despite the reduced use of weapons (as discussed in the previous section, the group context has been found to encourage violence (Morgan et al., 2012) and a number of studies find that group robberies are more violent than lone offences (Alarid et al., 2009; Porter & Alison, 2006a, 2006b).

## PROPERTY STOLEN

Small, valuable items (especially cash and mobile phones) are popularly stolen during robberies (Burrell, 2012; Flatley, 2017; Smith, 2003; Woodhams & Toye, 2007). This is not surprising given that these are the types of items that people commonly carry around with them. Furthermore, these items have been described as "hot products" within criminology research literature (Clarke, 1999). Hot products display "CRAVED" characteristics—i.e. they are concealable, removable, available, valuable, enjoyable, and disposable—making them attractive to thieves (Clarke, 1999; Clarke & Eck, 2003; Wellsmith & Burrell, 2005). Thus, the theft of items with these characteristics represents a common trend in property crime including robbery (Monk et al., 2010). As fashions change and technology advances, the specific items which are stolen may vary but all are likely to fit into the CRAVED criteria. For example, the way we pay for things is changing with a move away from cash towards debit/credit cards. Combined with the tap and PIN feature, this will increase the value of stealing cards going forward (Farrell & Tilley, 2021a, 2021b).

The value of goods stolen during the offence has increased over time with the estimated cost of goods stolen during a personal robbery to be £310 in 2000 (Brand & Price, 2000) but £1,030 by 2018 (Heeks et al., 2018). This is perhaps unsurprising as the value of property people carry has increased over time (e.g. people often carry mobile phones, music players, laptops, and/or other expensive devices with them) and what is stolen represents what is available.

There are different methods offenders can use to secure property from victims. For example, Burrell (2012) reports a range of behaviours from snatching/grabbing property to requesting or demanding the victim hands items to them. Some offenders searched victims and/or asked them to empty their pockets/bags. Verbal threats were also used along with display or use of weapon to encourage compliance.

## *Offender Adaptation*

Opportunities to commit crime can be impacted by technological advances (see Chapter 2). Sometimes this will mean the offenders need to adjust their methods of offending in order to be successful. For example, the introduction of new technology (e.g. car demobilisers) has made vehicles harder to steal. This means that the offenders need to adjust their methods. One example in this instance is to break into the victim's home to steal the car key (known as "car key burglaries" [Donkin & Wellsmith, 2006]). Alternatively, the car thief might escalate to robbery in order to steal the keys (known as carjacking [Burrell, 2012; Jacobs et al., 2003]). Offenders might also adapt to ongoing crime prevention measures—for example, changing where they offend if a new police patrol strategy is introduced. This raises concerns for the police as it could mean offending just moves to a new place rather than be prevented by interventions. There is a vast literature on crime displacement (see, for example, Johnson et al., 2014) and this has been seen in robbery (Hatten & Piza, 2021). However, how robbery is displaced is not inevitable (Johnson et al., 2014) or easily predictable (Hatten & Piza, 2021). For example, in some cases, displacement could result in less serious crime occurring (e.g. a shift from robbery to petty theft) (Guerette, 2009). Offender adaptation is not only something to consider for front-line crime prevention efforts, it can also affect analytical work. For example, it could prove challenging for behavioural crime linkage (see Chapter 5) if offenders change the way they behave across their crime series (Burrell et al., 2012).

## Conclusion

This chapter summarises some of the offence behaviours and methods used by robbers. Popular target groups have been identified along with the methods of approach used. Weapon display and use confirms the controlling and violent aspect of robbery offences. Property stolen is often small, high value goods especially cash. Offenders need to be adaptable to remain successful in their offending and a few examples of how they might adjust their methods to account for new trends are discussed.

## References

Alarid, L. F., Burton, V. S., & Hochstetler, A. L. (2009). Group and solo robberies: Do accomplices shape criminal form? *Journal of Criminal Justice, 37*, 1–9. https://doi.org/10.1016/j.jcrimjus.2008.12.001

Barker, M., Geraghty, J., Webb, B., & Key, T. (1993). *The prevention of street robbery* Police research group crime prevention unit series paper no. 44. Home Office. http://rds.homeoffice.gov.uk/rds/prgpdfs/fcpu44.pdf

Bernasco, W., & Block, R. (2011). Where offenders choose to attack: A discrete choice model of robberies in Chicago. *Criminology, 47*, 93–130.

Brand, S., & Price, R. (2000). *The economic and social costs of crime.* Home Office Research Study 217. Home Office.

Brown, I., Thompson, A., Pepper, I., & Ryan, M. (2019). *Mobile-enabled mobile phone snatches: A tale from two London boroughs.* European Law Enforcement Research Bulletin Nr. 18 (Winter 2019).

Burrell, A. (2012). *Behavioural case linkage in personal robbery* [PhD thesis, University of Leicester]. https://leicester.figshare.com/articles/thesis/Behavioural_Case_Linkage_in_Personal_Robbery/10147652/1

Burrell, A., Bull, R., & Bond, J. (2012). Linking personal robbery offences using offender behaviour. *Journal of Investigative Psychology and Offender Profiling*, *9*(3), 201–222. https://doi.org/10.1002/jip.1365

Burrell, A., Bull, R., Bond, J., & Herrington, G. (2015). Testing the impact of group offending on behavioural similarity in serial robbery. *Psychology, Crime & Law*, *21*(6), 551–569. https://doi.org/10.1080/1068316X.2014.999063

Caplan, J. M., Neudecker, C. H., Kennedy, L. W., Barnum, J. D., & Drawve, G. (2020). Tracking risk for crime throughout the day: An examination of Jersey City Robberies. *Criminal Justice Review*, 1–15. https://doi.org/10.1177/0734016820981628

Clarke, R. (1999). *Hot products: Understanding, anticipating, and reducing the demand for stolen goods*. Police Series Research Paper 112. Home Office.

Clarke, R. V., & Eck, J. (2003). *How to become a problem solving crime analyst*. Jill Dando Institute of Crime Science.

Commission on Race and Ethnic Disparities. (2021, April). *Crime and policing*. https://www.gov.uk/government/publications/the-report-of-the-commission-on-race-and-ethnic-disparities/crime-and-policing

Crown Prosecution Service. (2017). *Firearms*. https://www.cps.gov.uk/legal-guidance/firearms

da Silva, T., Woodhams, J., & Harkins, L. (2013). Heterogeneity within multiple perpetrator rapes: A national comparison of lone, duo, and 3+ perpetrator rapes. *Sexual Abuse*, *26*(6), 503–522. https://doi.org/10.1177/1079063213497805

de Hann, W., & Vos, J. (2003). A crying shame: The over-rationalized conception of man in the rational choice perspective. *Theoretical Criminology*, *7*(1), 29–54.

Deakin, J., Smithson, H., Spencer, J., & Medina-Ariza, J. (2007). Taxing on the streets: Understanding the methods and process of street robbery. *Crime Prevention and Community Safety*, *9*, 52–96. https://doi.org/10.1057/palgrave/cpps.8150033

Donkin, S., & Wellsmith, M. (2006). Cars stolen in burglaries: The Sandwell experience. *Security Journal*, *19*(1), 22–32. https://doi.org/10.1057/palgrave.sj.8350010

Drawve, G., Caplan, J., Kennedy, L. W., & Sarkos, J. (2020). Risk of robbery in a tourist destination: A monthly examination of Atlantic City, New Jersey. *Journal of Place Management and Development*, *13*(4), 429–446. https://doi.org/10.1108/JPMD-07-2019-0064

Farrell, G. & Tilley, N. (2021a). *Contactless card payment limits and crime rates after the pandemic*. UCL JDI Special Series on COVID-10: No. 26. https://www.ucl.ac.uk/jill-dando-institute/sites/jill-dando-institute/files/26_contactless_payments_final.pdf

Farrell, G. & Tilley, N. (2021b). *"Tap-and-PIN": Preventing crime and criminal careers from increased contactless payments.* UCL JDI Special Series on COVID-10: No. 28. https://www.ucl.ac.uk/jill-dando-institute/sites/jill_dando_institute/files/tap_and_pin_no_28.pdf

Felson, R. B., Baumer, E. P., & Messner, S. F. (2000). Acquaintance robbery. *Journal of Research in Crime and Delinquency, 37*(3), 284–305.

Flatley, J. (2017). *Overview of robbery and theft from the person: England and Wales.* Office for National Statistics. https://www.ons.gov.uk/peoplepopulationandcommunity/crimeandjustice/articles/overviewofrobberyandtheftfromtheperson/2017-07-20

Gerell, M. (2018). Bus stops and violence, are risky places really risky? *European Journal on Criminal Policy and Research, 24*(4), 351–371.

Goodwill, A. M., Stephens, S., Oziel, S., Yapp, J., & Bowes, N. (2012). A multidimensional latent classification of 'street robbery' offences. *Journal of Investigative Psychology and Offender Profiling, 9,* 93–109. https://doi.org/10.1002/jip.1351

Guerette, R. T. (2009). *Analyzing crime displacement and diffusion.* Problem-oriented guides for police problem-solving crime series no. 10. US Department of Justice. https://popcenter.asu.edu/sites/default/files/tools/pdfs/displacement.pdf

Hart, T. C., & Miethe, T. D. (2014). Street robbery and public bus stops: A case study of activity nodes and situational risk. *Security Journal, 27*(2), 180–193.

Hatten, D., & Piza, E. L. (2021). When crime moves and where does it go? Analyzing the spatial correlated of robbery incidents displaced by a place-based policing intervention. *Journal of Research in Crime and Delinquency,* 1–35. https://doi.org/10.1177/00224278211016030

Heeks, M., Reed, S., Tafsiri, M., & Prince, S. (2018). *The economic and social costs of crime.* Home Office Research Report 99. Home Office.

Home Office (2021). *Home Office Counting Rules for Recorded Crime: Robbery.* https://assets.publishing.service.gov.uk/government/uploads/system/uploads/attachment_data/file/977204/count-robbery-apr-2021.pdf

Jacobs, B. A. (2000). *Robbing drug dealers: Violence beyond the law.* Walter de Gruyter Inc.

Jacobs, B. A., Topalli, V., & Wright, R. (2003). Carjacking, streetlife and offender motivation. *British Journal of Criminology, 43,* 673–688.

Johnson, S. D., Guerette, R. T., & Bowers, K. (2014). Crime displacement: What we know, what we don't know, and what it means for crime reduction. *Journal of Experimental Psychology, 10,* 549–571.

Liu, L., Lan, M., Eck, J., & Lei King, E. (2020). Assessing the effects of bus stop relocation on street robbery. *Computers, Environment and Urban Systems, 80,* 101455. https://doi.org/10.1016/j.compenvurbsys.2019.101455

Loukaitou-Sideris, A. (1999). Hot spots of bus stop crime: The importance of environmental attributes. *Journal of the American Planning Association*, 65(4), 395–411.
Luckenbill, D. F. (1980). Patterns of force in robbery. *Deviant Behavior*, 1(3–4), 361–378. https://doi.org/10.1080/01639625.1980.9967533
Lundrigan, S., & Mueller-Johnson, K. (2013). Male stranger rape: A behavioral model of victim offender interaction. *Criminal Justice and Behavior*, 40(7), 763–783. https://doi.org/10.1177/0093854812474451
Monk, K. M., Heinonen, J. A., & Eck, J. E. (2010). *Street Robbery. Problem-Oriented Guides for Police Problem-Specific Guides Series No. 59.* https://cops.usdoj.gov/RIC/Publications/cops-p181-pub.pdf
Morgan, L., Brittain, B., & Welch, J. (2012). Multiple perpetrator sexual assault: How does it differ from assault by a single perpetrator? *Journal of Interpersonal Violence*, 27, 2415–2436. https://doi.org/10.1177/0886260511435 14
Office for National Statistics. (2020). *Nature of crime: Crime (data tables)*. https://www.ons.gov.uk/peoplepopulationandcommunity/crimeandjustice/datasets/natureofcrimerobbery
Porter, L. E., & Alison, L. J. (2006a). Behavioural coherence in group robbery: A circumplex model of offender and victim interactions. *Aggressive Behavior*, 32, 330–342. https://doi.org/10.1002/ab.20132
Porter, L. E., & Alison, L. J. (2006b). Examining group rape: A descriptive analysis of offender and victim behaviour. *European Journal of Criminology*, 3, 357–381. https://doi.org/10.1177/1477370806065586
Roncek, D., & Maier, P. (1991). Bars, blocks and crimes revisited: Linking the theory of routine activities to the empiricism of 'hot spots.' *Criminology*, 29(4), 725–753.
Smith, J. (2003). *The nature of personal robbery.* Home Office Research Study 254. Home Office. http://library.npia.police.uk/docs/hors254.pdf
Tilley, N., Smith, J., Finer, S., Erol, R., Charles, C., & Dobby, J. (2004). *Problem solving street crime: Practical lessons from the street crime initiative.* Home Office.
Tita, G. E., & Greenbaum, R. T. (2009). Crime, neighbourhoods, and units of analysis: Putting space into place. In In D. L. Weisburd, W. Bernasco, & G. J. N. Bruinsma (Eds.), *Putting crime in its place: Units of analysis in geographic criminology* (pp. 145–170). Springer.
van Wilsem, J. (2009). Urban streets as micro contexts to commit violence. In In D. L. Weisburd, W. Bernasco, & G. J. N. Bruinsma (Eds.), *Putting crime in its place: Units of analysis in geographic criminology* (pp. 199–216). Springer.
UK Parliament. (2007, June). *Nature and extent of young black people's over-representation.* https://publications.parliament.uk/pa/cm200607/cmselect/cmhaff/181/18105.htm

Wellsmith, M., & Burrell, A. (2005). The influence of purchase price and ownership levels on theft targets: The example of domestic burglary. *British Journal of Criminology, 45*, 741–764. https://doi.org/10.1093/bjc/azi003

Woodhams, J., & Toye, K. (2007). An empirical test of the assumptions of case linkage and offender profiling with serial commercial robberies. *Psychology, Public Policy, and Law, 13*, 59–85. https://doi.org/10.1037/1076-8971.13.1.59

Wüllenweber, S., & Burrell, A. (2020). Offence characteristics: A comparison of lone, duo, and 3+ perpetrator offences. *Psychology, Crime, and Law*. https://doi.org/10.1080/1068316X.2020.1780589

# CHAPTER 4

# Group Dynamics

**Abstract** Robbery is commonly committed by groups and this can create challenges for law enforcement. For example, members might have different motivations for committing the offence and some offenders talk about feeling peer pressuring and/or coerced into offending. This chapter explores theories of group behaviour and how this influences group offending. For example, the decision to commit crime, deciding who to commit crime with, the different roles individuals might have during the offence, risks of betrayal and capture, sharing the profits, etc. Consideration is given to how the group dynamic impacts on offending—for example, how this feeds into violence (or not if the group acts as a censor/regulates the behaviour of the wider group). The role of leadership is also discussed along with overlaps with gang offending.

**Keywords** Group dynamics · Group decision-making · Gang leadership · Group offending

## Introduction

We all belong to groups (Gençer, 2019)—often formed around mutual beliefs and shared traits (Roth et al., 2018)—and group membership impacts on processes such as decision-making and attitude formation.

This has clear relevance to investigating crime as offenders, like everyone, will be members of groups and this could influence if, when, and how they commit crime. For example, for young people, context can affect social interactions resulting in co-offending (Schaefer et al., 2014).

Research is often conducted using a single offender-single victim approach. However, this is not representative of all crime as sometimes the police will be looking for a group, especially in offences such as robbery. It is therefore important to understand how group dynamics impact on how offenders commit crime. Personal robbery is often committed by groups and so research with this crime type represents a good opportunity to explore the influence of group dynamics. This chapter will discuss overarching theory and explanations of how groups influence behaviour with specific examples of the impact on offending, especially in robbery.

## Group Dynamics

A group is two or more people who come together with a common purpose (Gençer, 2019). Group dynamics is the study or use of the processes involved when people in a group interact. These interactions influence the attitudes and behaviours of people—so much so that they might behave differently in a group to when they are alone (Gençer, 2019), for example, commit crime (Hochstetler et al., 2002). Group dynamics can relate to the ingroup (within social groups) or intergroup (between social groups) (Pettigrew & Tropp, 2011).

Ingroups are often formed around shared interests—for example, religion, politics, sports teams, or music. Within the group there is a state of interdependence where the behaviours, attitudes, opinions, and experiences of each individual member are collectively influenced and shaped by the group. Ingroups can experience intragroup conflict—this is where there is disharmony or disagreement between group members. Often these will be small-scale and are often resolved within the group as they share goals and ideals and so common ground can be found.

Social Identity Theory proposes that the groups we belong to create a sense of pride (Tajfel & Turner, 1979) and comparisons to other groups are used to build a positive image of our own social identities (Sanchez-Mazas & Licata, 2015). Comparisons are made to outgroups—i.e. groups that an individual or group does not identify with (Ashton & Bussu, 2020). Intergroups are identified where a behavioural relationship exists between one or more groups—for example, rivalries between supporters of different sports teams (or between gangs in a criminal context). Intergroup conflict starts with this process of comparison between individuals in one group (the ingroup) to individuals in another group (the outgroup). This comparison process is biased and subjective—in the process of such comparisons, an individual tends to (1) favour the ingroup over the outgroup, (2) exaggerate and overgeneralise the differences between the ingroup and the outgroup to enhance group distinctiveness, (3) minimise the perception of differences between ingroup members, and (4) remember more detailed and positive information about the ingroup, and more negative information about the outgroup. This emphasises the differences between groups (e.g. creating an "us and them" attitude) and makes intergroup conflict harder to resolve.

## Group Offending

Group/multiple perpetrator crimes are offences committed by two or more offenders (Burrell et al., 2015) against one or more victims and it is argued that group offending is an established "criminological fact" (Schaefer et al., 2014: 117). The prevalence of group offending varies by type of offence and is more strongly associated with certain types of crime (van Mastrigt & Farrington, 2009). It is common in predatory street crimes like robbery (Alarid et al., 2009; Deakin et al., 2007; Hochstetler, 2001; Weerman, 2003). The majority of robberies are committed by groups (e.g. Deakin et al., 2007; Kapardis, 1988; Walsh, 1986) and many offenders report they were persuaded to commit robbery by their co-offenders (Alarid et al., 2009).

Research has revealed that group offences are primarily committed by adolescents (e.g. Carrington, 2002; Conway & McCord, 2002; Porter & Alison, 2004, 2006b). This includes personal robbery which is typically committed by young males (Alarid et al., 2009; Burrell, 2012; Porter & Alison, 2006a, 2006c). Young offenders commonly have friends who engage in crime (Conway & McCord, 2002), and the attitudes and behaviours of friends have been found to be a significant determinant of whether a young person commits theft, assault, and vandalism (Hochstetler et al., 2002). This is supported by Ashton and Bussu (2020) whose interviews with young male offenders revealed some described being manipulated or coerced into criminal behaviour by peers. Such findings apply to both group and lone offending suggesting that it is not just the presence of the group but the indirect influences of friends' attitudes and behaviours that are relevant to the propensity to offend. This, in turn, suggests that it is not the group that encourages crime, but the deviant peers within it. Having said this, behaviour and attitudes can become more extreme in group settings (Porter & Alison, 2006c) and young offenders are more likely to commit serious crimes when in the presence of accomplices (Alarid et al., 2009). Group offending typically declines with age (Alarid et al., 2009; Carrington, 2002; McGloin et al., 2008; van Mastrigt & Farrington, 2009), and it is suggested that as offenders age they are probably less susceptible to the influence of others (Hochstetler et al., 2002). Older offenders are also more likely to recognise that accomplices increase risks and reduce rewards (Alarid et al., 2009) which might shift an individual from group to lone offending later in life.

As young people become more embedded in the group, they lose their sense of individuality and may take on the collective behaviours of the group (Hauffe & Porter, 2009). The group dynamic and the loss of self-awareness act to facilitate aggressive and immoral actions in groups. People are also more likely to "show off" to their peers and/or protect their reputation in the group context (Alarid et al., 2009), leading individuals to behave somewhat differently when in a group than when they are alone. In addition, behaviour and attitudes can become more extreme in group settings (Porter & Alison, 2006c)—for example, be more likely to involve physical violence (Alarid et al., 2009; Porter & Alison, 2006a, 2006b). It has also been reported that previously non-violent offenders who commit their first group offences with violent accomplices are at an increased risk of continuing with violent crime (Conway & McCord, 2002), indicating the group context can act as a pathway into more serious offending. Research has also demonstrated that people base their actions on previous experience (Juliusson et al., 2005) and so offenders may adopt methods they have learned from others.

The group context can influence behaviour as psychological processes allow people to be persuaded to behave in a way they might not otherwise. In an offending context, the group allows the individuals within it to intimidate in numbers (Porter & Alison, 2006b) and to experience diffused responsibility (Alarid et al., 2009; Porter & Alison, 2006b) which can reduce their individual capacity to enforce their own moral sense of right and wrong. The fact that groups are more likely to target victims they do not know (Alarid et al., 2009) may also work to depersonalise the victim which could act as a facilitator for violence (e.g. you are less likely to care about harming someone who has been depersonalised).

It is theorised, therefore, that the group context provides a comfort zone for offending, allowing individuals to feel anonymous (Alarid et al., 2009; Hauffe & Porter, 2009). This anonymity and the resulting loss of identity and self-control is called de-individuation (Woodhams et al., 2019), with greater de-individuation effects expected as the group size increases (Postmes & Spears, 1998).

### *Selecting Co-offenders*

Weerman (2003) describes co-offending as a process of social exchange where offenders must be willing to co-offend and be attractive to each other as co-offenders. A key element of co-offending is trust (Ashton & Bussu, 2020). However, identifying trustworthy co-offenders can be challenging as offending is a risky endeavour (Schaefer et al., 2014). In short, a lack of trust can influence whether people decide and/or continue to co-offend (Schaefer et al., 2014) and so it is important that co-offenders build trust to enhance the chances of success. There are different ways in which trust operates—(1) individualised—which is based on expectations of how co-offenders will behave (e.g. based on past experiences with that individual), (2) reputation (i.e. a more widely held and known view about the activities of a particular person), and (3) generalisations (i.e. expectations of how people from particular groups might behave) (van Lampe & Johansen, 2004). Underpinning all of these is knowledge of the individual and this is used to decide if they can be trusted to commit crime with.

With reference to robbery, Alarid et al. (2009) report male robbers prefer co-offenders who are similar in age and ethnicity with allegiance to the group understood through shared experiences and background. It has also been reported that street gangs and peer groups are often people from the same housing estate or postcode (Ashton & Bussu, 2020) indicating some common ground in terms of geography.

It is not unusual for offenders to limit the number of accomplices. For example, 52% of robbers interviewed by Alarid et al. (2009) only had one co-offender, and 54% of the robbery groups examined by Porter and Alison (2006c) were made up of two offenders. Keeping the number of co-offenders down reduces the number of people to divide the proceeds with (Weerman, 2003). It also reduces the risk of capture through member disloyalty (Weerman, 2003). Ashton and Bussu (2020) report some offenders (adolescent males) report being involved in multiple groups depending on the offence they were committing. This mirrors earlier findings by Warr (1996) who reported that offenders are less likely to use the same accomplices for different types of crime. This suggests a form of group specialisation for offending. Co-offenders expand criminal opportunities (Alarid et al., 2009; Porter & Alison, 2006b) through specialist knowledge (e.g. of target location or weakness), skills (e.g. breaking into a vehicle), and/or access (e.g. if they work as a security officer at a bank). Having said this, aside from target selection, it is unlikely that any degree of specialist knowledge is needed to commit personal robbery (Reale et al., 2021), and so personal robbers may be more fluid in their selection of co-offenders.

## *Group Stability*

The evidence for group stability is mixed. Crime groups (robbery or otherwise) are often characterised as short-lived, loosely associated, and transitory (Carrington, 2002; Weerman, 2003). The same group may not commit more than one offence together and Weerman (2003) reported that offending groups typically change after one criminal event. Furthermore, McGloin et al. (2008) report that young offenders do not tend to "re-use" co-offenders and so argued that they found little evidence of stability in the selection of co-offenders. However, Burrell (2012) argues their data could be interpreted differently as, although more than half of offenders showed no stability, 39% showed some, and 2% showed perfect stability. Furthermore, as the research used official data rather than self-reports, it is likely the level of offender stability has been underestimated (because some offenders are not caught so the co-offender data is missing). The fact the study showed frequent offenders show a greater propensity to recycle co-offenders only supports this point. Finally, it does not appear that their study controlled for offence type which may have impacted on the level of co-offender stability. Overall, although the group as a whole may not be stable, it is likely that some relationships and connections within groups will persist (McGloin et al., 2008), for example, within criminal gangs where bonds between some members are reported to be very strong and even family-like in nature (Howell, 1998). Furthermore, whilst some opportunist offenders may use a variety of co-offenders (McGloin et al., 2008), other offenders have small social networks and are likely to select the same co-offenders repeatedly, particularly when they commit multiple offences within a short timeframe (Warr, 1996).

## Characteristics of Group and Lone Offending

Research on group offending has highlighted a number of characteristics that differ between group and lone offending. In robbery, offenders might find the presence of co-offenders reassuring. For example, because it reduces the fear of victim resistance and chances of being caught (Alarid et al., 2009).

### Offenders

Burrell (2012) reports group offenders are typically younger (average age 17–18) than lone offenders (average age 20–22). However, the age ranges were similar across group and lone offences indicating that at least some very young offenders (aged 10–12 years) commit robberies alone and some older offenders offend in groups (Burrell, 2012).

### Target Selection

The majority of personal robbery, particularly group offences, is male on male (Burrell, 2012). Where females are targeted, this is more likely to be by a lone offender than by a group (Burrell, 2012). Groups of robbers typically target lone victims (e.g. Burrell, 2012; Porter & Alison, 2004) but are more likely to target a group than a lone offender (Alarid et al., 2009; Burrell, 2012). Groups tend to target younger victims than lone offenders (e.g. Morgan et al., 2012). For example, Burrell (2012) reports a mean age of 20 for victims of group offences (in two samples of robbery offences) compared to 25 or 27 for victims of lone offenders.

Interestingly, Alarid et al. (2009) found that group offending did not impact on victim selection and groups did not choose riskier targets. This indicates that there are other factors influencing victim selection; for example, offenders may respond to a spontaneous opportunity or the offence is targeted against a particular person (e.g. as a means of debt collecting or gang related). It could also be that different members expand the groups awareness space (i.e. locations offenders become familiar with during their day to day activities) thus potentially helping them to identify more opportunities to commit crime. This may be why Burrell's (2012) groups typically travel further to commit their offences than lone offenders (e.g. in West Midlands group offenders travelled 2,214 metres from their home address on average compared to 1,522 metres for lone offenders).

### *Planning*

Groups are more likely to plan their offence, even if this is quite basic (Alarid et al., 2009)—for example, decide roles. This makes sense for some crime types where individual members of the group may be assigned roles (e.g. robbery). Even if the robbery is spontaneous, the offenders may need to discuss, however briefly, the method of approach. For example, if a group decides to rob a person they may need to plan each person's role in the crime. This is in contrast to the lone offender who only needs to consider his/her own actions. Harding et al. (2019) found planned offences were associated with more organised groups.

### *Violence*

Group offenders have strength in numbers which can be used to control the victim (Porter & Alison, 2006b), if only through intimidation rather than physical violence. The lone offender, on the other hand, is more likely to need a weapon to achieve the same level of control, and as such, the weapon could be a substitute for an accomplice (Alarid et al., 2009). However, groups commit more violent offences than lone offenders (Conway & McCord, 2002) and the group offence itself is more violent (Morgan et al., 2012). Group offences are more likely to involve physical violence (Alarid et al., 2009; Porter & Alison, 2006a, 2006b), and there is evidence that young people are more likely to behave violently (e.g. shooting, stabbing, punching, kicking) during a group offence (Conway & McCord 1995 cited in Conway & McCord, 2002).

Group offences are more likely to involve multiple acts of violence within the offence (e.g. Hauffe and Porter (2009) found 78% of rapes committed by a group included multiple acts of violence compared to 60% of rapes by lone offenders). The robbery group is less likely to use weapons (Burrell, 2012) but the most serious injuries are associated with group offences (Alarid et al., 2009; Burrell, 2012). There is little difference between group and lone offences for "slight injury" (Alarid et al., 2009). Finally, previously non-violent offenders who commit their first group offences with violent accomplices are at an increased risk of continuing with violent crime (Conway & McCord, 2002) indicating the importance of acknowledging the impact of the group.

## Does Size Matter?

The research discussed so far demonstrates how being alone or with a group when committing a crime can shape the criminal process. However, groups are diverse! It is therefore important to consider whether the size of the group impacts on offender decision-making and, if so, how. Research shows that duos show behaviours dissimilar from those in bigger groups, resulting from different group dynamics (e.g. da Silva et al., 2013; Harkins & Dixon, 2010; Park & Kim, 2016). Furthermore, it is clear that group dynamics are different in different sized groups—for example, there is one relationship in a duo, 3 pairwise relationships in a trio, 6 in a foursome, etc. This is important for the criminal process as where one damaged relationship would destroy a duo it is likely a larger group would survive (Moreland, 2010). Thus, it is argued that duos should be investigated separately to larger groups (Moreland, 2010).

### *Learning from the Sex Offending Literature*

Some essential work on group offending has been conducted in relation to sex offending. da Silva and colleagues (2013) analysed a sample of 336 allegations of rape in the UK and found significant differences between rapes committed by lone, duo, and 3+ perpetrator groups. Firstly, there were differences in offender demographics (e.g. lone offenders were significantly older than duos who were, in turn, older than 3+ perpetrator group offenders). Secondly, they found differences in offending behaviours including approach, locations of initial contact, and vehicle use. They also identified differences in assault and release of victims as well as verbal themes, use of precautions (such as covering mouth, blocking victim escape), and the types of sexual acts performed (e.g. lone offenders kissed victims more often than 3+ group offenders). Park and Kim (2016) drew on da Silva et al.'s (2013) work, sampling 340 sexual assault cases from North Korea comparing offender characteristics, victim characteristics, and offence behaviours between lone, duo, and 3+ perpetrator groups. Although the variables differed from da Silva et al. (2013)—for example, Park and Kim (2016) did not have information on sexual acts committed during the offence—they did also demonstrate differences between lone, duo, and 3+ perpetrator offences. In particular, they found differences in offender age, marital status, and employment, as well as differences in victim–offender relationships (e.g. lone offenders were significantly more likely to assault a stranger). Differences in offence processes were also observed—for example, group offences were more likely to be planned than lone offences. Overall, research has revealed that the execution of the crime, as well as offender and victim characteristics, is different depending on the size of the offender group.

Research on offence behaviours in groups of varying sizes has also demonstrated that the relationship between violence and groups is not straightforward. For example, greater de-individuation effects are expected as the group size increases (Postmes & Spears, 1998). Thus, it is perhaps not surprising that group offending is associated with increased use of violence and injuries in victims (as compared to lone offending) (Alarid et al., 2009; Hauffe & Porter, 2009). However, there has also been research which indicates that larger groups are not necessarily associated with more violence. For example, Woodhams et al. (2019) conducted research with a sample of 71 accounts of multiple perpetrator rape (MPR) by 189 offenders against lone females. Victim accounts were coded for leader, follower, and victim actions and offences rated as high or low non-sexual aggression. Woodhams and colleagues (2019) found hostility towards victims decreased as group size increased which is contrary to what was predicted (i.e. that de-individuation would mean individual group members would feel anonymous in a group and therefore behave in a more hostile way). This suggests increasing group size does not reduce the ability of the group to self-regulate aggression. Similar findings have been reported in research on bystander intervention. Levine et al. (2011) found the tendency for people to take conciliatory actions which lead to a de-escalation in violence increased as the group size increased. This study focused on third party intervention where two antagonists fought in the presence of at least two third parties rather than offender behaviour but still demonstrates how the group dynamic operates to de-escalate violence.

## Groups, Duos, and Lone Robbery Offenders

The research on sex offending has revealed that offence behaviours can differ depending on the size of the offending group (Wüllenweber & Burrell, 2020). It is also clear that the relationship between group size and violence is not clear-cut. Robbery is a predominantly group offence (Burrell, 2012; Deakin et al., 2007) with varying group sizes (Shubak Tillyer & Tillyer, 2015; Wüllenweber & Burrell, 2020). Thus, robbery presents an ideal opportunity to investigate the impact of different sized groups on offending. Furthermore, understanding these differences could support the development of crime prevention initiatives and investigative strategies (Wüllenweber & Burrell, 2020).

Wüllenweber and Burrell (2020) examined the offence characteristics of robbery committed by different sized groups, namely lone, duos, and groups of 3 or more (from now on referred to as 3+ perpetrator offences). Data from 1,574 personal robbery offences, involving over 3,800 offenders, was provided by West Midlands Police (UK). The number of offenders ranged from 1 to 31 per incident although the most common group size for 3+ perpetrator offences was 3. Two-fifths of offences were committed by lone offenders ($n = 647$; 41%) with a quarter committed by duos ($n = 409$, 26%), and the remainder committed by groups of 3+ perpetrators ($n = 518$, 33%).

The results revealed significant differences between the three group sizes across a range of variables including offender age, victim age, approach styles used, controlling behaviours, weapon use, alcohol use, violence, injury, and carjacking (i.e. robbery of a motor vehicle using threat or force). These differences can be telling about group processes. For example, a negative correlation was found between group size and the surprise approach which is indicative of the need for lone offenders to overwhelm their victim quickly (Wüllenweber & Burrell, 2020). Groups, on the other hand, are able to control the victim(s) using the size of the group itself (i.e. multiple people) (Porter & Alison, 2006b), and so it is not surprising that this research also found group offences were more likely to involve physical violence (Wüllenweber & Burrell, 2020) which would align with how we would expect depersonalisation to operate in a group setting. The results also revealed that carjacking was associated with group offending (duos and 3+ perpetrator offences) which makes sense if this type of modus operandi requires more expertise and/or the need for co-offenders to achieve success (Jacobs et al., 2003). This was a small subsample though (carjacking accounted for 2.4% of duo offences, 2.5% of 3+ perpetrator offences, and just 0.6% of lone offences) and so it is difficult to draw firm conclusions from this. Overall, the research did demonstrate a number of differences between lone, duo, and 3+ perpetrator offences, many of which are easily explained by group dynamics, which suggests that the size of the group does matter in offence decision-making and execution.

## Leadership

Research has found a level of behavioural coherence in group offending, specifically that robbery offenders within the same group behave in a homogenous fashion (Porter & Alison, 2006a). It is suggested that this is due to group members following a leader. Woodhams et al. (2019) found leader behaviour to have a significant effect on group violence. Specifically, that leader influence is moderated by mimicry of the leaders' hostile (or submissive) behaviours (e.g. in high aggression rapes, the leaders' acts of hostility are encouraged by peers' use of dominance towards the victim). This suggests followers create a social norm that allows the leader to define the behavioural choices of the group. For example, Porter and Alison (2006a) suggested that behavioural coherence was due to group members copying a leader. They argued that the leader not only encourages other group members to offend but that, when they do, members imitate the behaviours of the leader. Their further research (Porter & Alison, 2006c) supported this hypothesis with the finding that, in most cases, one member of the robbery group could be identified as the potential leader; i.e. they exhibited more leadership behaviour than their co-offenders (103 out of 105 groups or 98%; note that two leaders were identified in the remaining two cases). Although it was reported that other group members displayed influential behaviour during the crime, this was to a lesser degree than the leader. Thus, if groups always follow with the same leader, it would be expected that the behaviours displayed during each offence would remain consistent across a series of incidents. This research demonstrates how group dynamics can shape the criminal process (Wüllenweber & Burrell, 2020).

## Gangs and Robbery

It is impossible to talk about group offending without considering gangs. There are many definitions of gangs—and much discussion about the differences between them (e.g. urban street gangs versus organised crime groups)—though there is not space to discuss the nuances of such descriptions in depth here (see Ashton and Bussu [2020] for a useful discussion). Suffice to say that, in this context, discussion of gangs includes instances where a (semi) organised group of people commit personal robbery offences.

Gangs are associated with committing personal robbery offences (Ashton & Bussu, 2020; Harding et al., 2019; Whittaker et al., 2020); for example, as a way to advance their social status within the group (Harding et al., 2019). Ashton and Bussu (2020) interviewed 15 young men (aged 14–18 years) who had been involved in gangs. They found that, where the group commits the offence, relatively few gang members (typically 2–3) are needed for a robbery in comparison to other gang activity (e.g. fighting). The research also found street gang members were often identified as street robbers, with one participant reporting that these offences were often opportunistic and committed because young people were living in poverty (Ashton & Bussu, 2020). Harding et al. (2019)—who interviewed 42 current and ex-offenders about the relationship between gang organisation and street robbery—also found some gang robbery was opportunistic. This was associated with territorial young street gangs who tended to commit offences on their own even if associates were nearby offering support or back up. More organised groups were more organised in their robbery as well and participants reported robbery might form the gang's main occupation (Harding et al., 2019).

Gangs will target their own criminal peers, non-criminal peer groups (e.g. young people out clubbing), and/or the general public (Harding et al., 2019). Robbery by gangs often occurs in the illegitimate economy (Harding et al., 2019; Jacobs, 2000). For example, targeting of other offenders such as drug dealers (Harding et al., 2019; Jacobs, 2000).

An interesting point to note with gangs/organised crime groups is that their primary motivation is money (El Siwi, 2018; Lavorgna, 2015). Therefore, if robbery becomes less profitable or another crime becomes more profitable, the prevalence of offending should reduce (Whittaker et al., 2020). For example, goods can only be translated into cash if offenders are sufficiently networked with people who can fence (i.e. sell on) stolen goods (Harding et al., 2019). Participants in Whittaker et al. (2020) report that changes in the value of stolen property are meaning gang members are turning away from this type of offence (e.g. towards drug distribution instead). There are also moves by organised crime groups towards more cyber-enabled offending (Lavorgna, 2015) which could shift focus away from robbery as well.

## Conclusion

Group dynamics are associated with everyday activities. Peer influence is associated with the general propensity to offend (whether alone or in a group) (Burrell et al., 2015). For some people, group membership and activities might impact on their offending behaviour (e.g. whether they choose to offend, how they commit their offences, etc.). Furthermore, research does indicate that group dynamics impact on offending (e.g. different modus operandi are associated with group versus lone offences). However, although group dynamics have a role to play in offending, it is not as simple as group versus lone offending. The size of the group matters as the dynamics will be different. Roles and relationships (e.g. leaders, followers) are important. In particular, it is argued that group dynamics and peer influence are the best explanation for violence in multiple perpetrator rape (Woodhams et al., 2019). Given the findings of Porter and Alison (2006a, 2006c), it is argued that the same is likely to apply to robbery as well. It is therefore important to consider the potential impact of the group on robbery rates and/or how robbery is committed locally as understanding group dynamics can facilitate investigations (e.g. the development of new crime prevention tactics, or to feed into the interpretation of data). Positively, research has demonstrated that intergroup contact can reduce prejudice which can lead to attitude change (Pettigrew & Tropp, 2011) indicating proactive action can be taken to overcome group conflict.

## References

Alarid, L. F., Burton, V. S., & Hochstetler, A. L. (2009). Group and solo robberies: Do accomplices shape criminal form? *Journal of Criminal Justice*, 37, 1–9. https://doi.org/10.1016/j.jcrimjus.2008.12.001

Ashton, S.-A., & Bussu, A. (2020). Peer groups, street gangs and organised crime in the narratives of adolescent male offenders. *Journal of Criminal Psychology, 10*(4), 277–292. https://doi.org/10.1108/JCP-06-2020-0020

Burrell, A. (2012). *Behavioural case linkage in personal robbery* [PhD thesis, University of Leicester]. https://leicester.figshare.com/articles/thesis/Behavioural_Case_Linkage_in_Personal_Robbery/10147652/1

Burrell, A., Bull, R., Bond, J., & Herrington, G. (2015). Testing the impact of group offending on behavioural similarity in serial robbery. *Psychology, Crime & Law, 21*(6), 551–569. https://doi.org/10.1080/1068316X.2014.999063

Carrington, P. J. (2002). Group crime in Canada. *Canadian Journal of Criminology, 44*, 277–315.

Conway, K. P., & McCord, J. (2002). A longitudinal examination of the relation between co-offending with violent accomplices and violent crime. *Aggressive Behavior, 28*, 97–108. https://doi.org/10.1002/ab.90011

da Silva, T., Woodhams, J., & Harkins, L. (2013). Heterogeneity within multiple perpetrator rapes: A national comparison of lone, duo, and 3+ perpetrator rapes. *Sexual Abuse, 26*(6), 503–522. https://doi.org/10.1177/1079063213497805

Deakin, J., Smithson, H., Spencer, J., & Medina-Ariza, J. (2007). Taxing on the streets: Understanding the methods and process of street robbery. *Crime Prevention and Community Safety, 9*, 52–96. https://doi.org/10.1057/palgrave/cpps.8150033

El Siwi, Y. (2018). Terrorism, organised crime and threat mitigation in a globalised world. *Journal of Financial Crime, 25*(4), 951–961. https://doi.org/10.1108/JFC-02-2017-0015

Gençer, H. (2019). Group dynamics and behaviour. *Universial Journal of Educational Research, 7*(1), 223–229. https://doi.org/10.13189/ujer.2019.070128

Harding, S., Deuchar, R., Densley, J., & McLean, R. (2019). A typology of street robbery and gang organization: Insights from qualitative research in Scotland. *British Journal of Criminology, 59*(4), 879–897.

Harkins, L., & Dixon, L. (2010). Sexual offending in groups: An evaluation. *Aggression and Violent Behavior, 15*(2), 87–99. https://doi.org/10.1016/j.avb.2009.08.006

Hauffe, S., & Porter, L. (2009). An interpersonal comparison of lone and group rape offences. *Psychology, Crime, and Law, 15*, 469–491. https://doi.org/10.1080/10683160802409339

Hochstetler, A. (2001). Opportunities and decisions: Interactional dynamics in robbery and burglary groups. *Criminology, 39*(3), 737–763.

Hochstetler, A., Copes, H., & DeLisi, M. (2002). Differential association in group and solo offending. *Journal of Criminal Justice, 30*, 559–566.

Howell, J. C. (1998). *Youth gangs: An overview*. US Department of Justice: Office of Juvenile Justice and Delinquency Prevention. https://www.ce-credit.com/articles/101181/167249.pdf

Jacobs, B. A. (2000). *Robbing drug dealers: Violence beyond the law*. Walter de Gruyter Inc.

Jacobs, B. A., Topalli, V., & Wright, R. (2003). Carjacking, streetlife and offender motivation. *British Journal of Criminology, 43*, 673–688.

Juliusson, E. Á., Karlsson, N., & Gärling, T. (2005). Weighing the past and future in decision making. *European Journal of Cognitive Psychology, 17*, 561–575. https://doi.org/10.1080/09541440440000159

Kapardis, A. (1988). One hundred convicted armed robbers in Melbourne: Myths and reality. In D. Challinger (Ed.), *Armed robbery* (AIC Seminar Proceedings, No. 26). Australian Institute of Criminology.

Lavorgna, A. (2015). Organised crime goes online: Realities and challenges. *Journal of Money Laundering Control, 18*(2), 153–168. https://doi.org/10.1108/JMLC-10-2014-0035

Levine, M., Taylor, P., & Best, R. (2011). Third parties, violence, and conflict resolution: The role of group size and collective action in the microregulation of violence. *Psychological Science*, 406–412.

McGloin, J. M., Sullivan, C. J., Piquero, A. R., & Bacon, S. (2008). Investigating the stability of co-offending and co-offenders among a sample of youthful offenders. *Criminology, 41*, 155–188.

Moreland, R. L. (2010). Are dyads really groups? *Small Group Research, 41*(2), 251–267. https://doi.org/10.1177/1046496409358618

Morgan, L., Brittain, B., & Welch, J. (2012). Multiple perpetrator sexual assault: How does it differ from assault by a single perpetrator? *Journal of Interpersonal Violence, 27*, 2415–2436. https://doi.org/10.1177/0886260511433514

Park, J., & Kim, S. (2016). Group size does matter: Differences among sexual assaults committed by lone, double, and groups of three or more perpetrators. *Journal of Sexual Aggression, 22*(3), 342–354. https://doi.org/10.1080/13552600.2016.1144801

Pettigrew, T. F., & Tropp, L. R. (2011). *When groups meet: The dynamics of intergroup contact*. Psychology Press.

Porter, L. E., & Alison, L. J. (2004). Behavioural coherence in violent group activity: An interpersonal model of sexually violent gang behaviour. *Aggressive Behavior, 30*, 449–468. https://doi.org/10.1002/ab.20047

Porter, L. E., & Alison, L. J. (2006a). Behavioural coherence in group robbery: A circumplex model of offender and victim interactions. *Aggressive Behavior, 32*, 330–342. https://doi.org/10.1002/ab.20132

Porter, L. E., & Alison, L. J. (2006b). Examining group rape: A descriptive analysis of offender and victim behaviour. *European Journal of Criminology, 3*, 357–381. https://doi.org/10.1177/1477370806065586

Porter, L. E., & Alison, L. J. (2006c). Leadership and hierarchies in criminal groups: Scaling degrees of leader behaviour in group robbery. *Legal & Criminological Psychology, 11*, 234–265. https://doi.org/10.1348/135532 50568692

Postmes, T., & Spears, R. (1998). Deindividuation and antinormative behaviour: A meta-analysis. *Psychological Bulletin, 123*(3), 238–259. https://doi.org/10.1037/0033-2909.123.3.238

Reale, K. S., Beauregard, E., & Chopin, J. (2021). Comparing the crime-commission process involved in sexual burglary and sexual robbery. *Criminal Justice and Behavior.* Advance online publication. https://doi.org/10.1177/00938548211023541

Roth, J., Steffens, M. C., & Vignoles, V. L. (2018). Group membership, group change, and intergroup attitudes: A recategorization model based on cognitive consistency principles. *Frontiers in Psychology, 9*, 479. https://doi.org/10.3389/fpsyg.2018.00479

Sanchez-Mazas, M., & Licata, L. (2015). Xenophobia: Social psychological aspects. In J. D. Wright (Ed.), *International Encyclopedia of the Social & Behavioral Sciences.* (2nd ed., pp. 802–807). Elsevier.

Schaefer, D. R., Rodriguez, N., & Decker, S. H. (2014). Role of neighborhood context in youth co-offending. *Criminology, 52*(1), 117–139.

Shubak Tillyer, M., & Tillyer, R. (2015). Maybe I should do this alone: A comparison of solo and co-offending robbery outcomes. *Justice Quarterly, 32*(6), 1064–1088.

Tajfel, H. & Turner, J. C. (1979). An integrative theory of intergroup conflict. In W. G. Austin, & S. Worchel (Eds.), *The social psychology of intergroup relations* (pp. 33–48). Brooks/Cole.

van Lampe, K., & Johansen, P. O. (2004). Organized Crime and Trust:: On the conceptualization and empirical relevance of trust in the context of criminal networks. *Global Crime, 6*(2), 159–184. https://doi.org/10.1080/174405 70500096734

van Mastrigt, S. B., & Farrington, D. P. (2009). Co-offending, age, gender, and crime type: The implications for criminal justice policy. *British Journal of Criminology, 46*(4), 552–573. https://doi.org/10.1093/bjc/azp021

Walsh, D. (1986). *Heavy business: Commercial burglary and robbery.* Routledge.

Warr, M. (1996). Organization and instigation in delinquent groups. *Criminology, 34*, 11–37.

Weerman, F. M. (2003). Co-offending as social exchange: Explaining characteristics of co-offending. *British Journal of Criminology, 43*, 398–416.

Whittaker, A., Densley, J., Cheston, L., Tyrell, T., Higgins, M., Felix-Baptiste, C., & Havard, T. (2020). Reluctant gangsters revisited: The evolution of gangs from postcodes to profits. *European Journal on Criminal Policy and Research, 26*, 1–22. https://doi.org/10.1007/s10610-019-09408-4

Woodhams, J., Taylor, P., & Cooke, C. (2019). Multiple perpetrator rape: Is perpetrator violence the result of victim resistance, deindividuation, or leader-follower dynamics? *Psychology of Violence, 10*(1), 120–129. https://doi.org/10.1037/vio0000255

Wüllenweber, S., & Burrell, A. (2020). Offence characteristics: A comparison of lone, duo, and 3+ perpetrator offences. *Psychology, Crime, and Law.* https://doi.org/10.1080/1068316X.2020.1780589

# CHAPTER 5

# Behavioural Crime Linkage

**Abstract** Research has shown that the majority of offences are committed by a minority of offenders. Therefore, any method to help identify prolific/serial offenders is of benefit to the police. Behavioural Crime Linkage (BCL) is a method of identifying series of offences committed by the same person(s) using the behaviour displayed during the offence. This can include, but is not limited to, target selection, control and weapon use, approach, property stolen, and temporal and spatial trends. This chapter will explain the theoretical framework for BCL and common methods for testing the accuracy of this method (e.g. logistic regression, Receiver Operating Characteristic). The chapter will then outline how BCL has been applied in robbery. It will discuss how the success of BCL is influenced by factors such as type of location (e.g. urban versus rural) and group offending (e.g. can you link offences committed by groups?). This chapter will draw heavily on the PhD research of the author but will cite other literature (e.g. evidence to support the theoretical framework for BCL) where relevant.

**Keywords** Behavioural crime linkage · Crime linkage · Robbery

# Introduction

## Crime Linkage

Identifying crime series, and attributing these to a single offender/group of offenders, is essential for police investigators (Bennell et al., 2009; Sorochinski & Salfati, 2010) as it allows them to implement more efficient investigative strategies (Labuschagne, 2012) such as pooling information from multiple crime scenes to generate investigative leads (Bennell et al., 2009). Links between offences can be established using forensic evidence (such as DNA or footwear), however, such evidence is not always present at a crime scene (Ewart et al., 2005). Furthermore, where forensic evidence is collected, this can be expensive and time-consuming to process (Tjin-A-Tsoi, 2013) and so police officers need other avenues to explore in live investigations. One opportunity is to identify the behaviours exhibited during the offence and use these to attribute series of crimes to a common offender. This is called behavioural crime linkage.

The feasibility of behavioural crime linkage rests on two assumptions; behavioural consistency (i.e. that offenders behave in a consistent way across their offences) (Canter, 1995) and behavioural distinctiveness (i.e. that offenders behave differently from other offenders) (Goodwill & Alison, 2006). Both assumptions need to be met in order for crime linkage to work; i.e. the assumptions allow individual offender's crimes to be (1) linked together, and (2) distinguished from the offences committed by others. Evidence for behavioural consistency and/or distinctiveness has been found for a range of crime types including vehicle crime (Tonkin et al., 2008), burglary (Bennell & Canter, 2002; Markson et al., 2010), commercial robbery (Woodhams & Toye, 2007), sexual assault (Grubin et al., 2001), homicide (Salfati et al., 2014), and arson (Ellingwood et al., 2013; Santtila et al., 2004). There is also evidence for behavioural consistency and distinctiveness in personal robbery as evidenced in PhD work by Burrell (2012) and subsequent papers from the thesis (e.g. Burrell et al., 2012, 2015).

Aside from assumption testing, research has also focused on identifying the behaviours (or combinations of behaviours) which are the most useful for making linking decisions. Behaviours which have consistently been found to be useful for linking include inter-crime distance (i.e. geographical distance between crime scenes) (e.g. Markson et al., 2010; Tonkin et al., 2008), temporal proximity (e.g. number of days between offences) (e.g. Burrell et al., 2012), and control (e.g. Burrell et al., 2012).

## Challenges for Linking Robberies

There are several issues which could negatively impact the ability to link robbery offences using behaviour. Firstly, personal robbery is commonly committed by groups of offenders (Burrell et al., 2012; Smith, 2003), and it is possible that group dynamics might impact on how the offence is committed. This could affect behavioural consistency reducing the potential to accurately link offences committed by groups. For example, Alarid et al. (2009) report that group offences are more likely to be planned. Furthermore, group offences are more likely to target multiple victims (Hauffe & Porter, 2009) and be more violent (e.g. Porter & Alison, 2006b). However, UK-based research on behavioural coherence has found that robbers tend to behave in a homogenous way when they operate in a group (Porter & Alison, 2006a). Thus, although the potential impact of group dynamics has been identified as a key factor to consider in linking research on personal robbery, if individuals within a group behave similarly it may still be possible to link group offences.

A second issue which might impact on the ability to link crimes using behaviour is offender learning and adaptation. As offenders learn what is effective (Keppel, 1995), attempt to work around crime prevention measures (Tilley et al., 2004), and gain confidence (Douglas & Munn, 1992), it is possible that their modus operandi (i.e. the way they commit the crime) will evolve (Yokota & Watanabe, 2002). This lack of behavioural consistency would create a challenge for crime linkage. However, research on robbery has found that many offenders develop a consistent method of committing their offences (Deakin et al., 2007) suggesting crime linkage would still be feasible.

## Methods Used in Crime Linkage

Research in crime linkage has utilised different approaches. For example, some researchers use a pairwise approach to predict whether two crimes are linked or not. Other researchers use ranking approaches to predict series membership (i.e. which series does the index offence belong to) or compare all crimes in the dataset to an index offence to try to find linked cases. There are also a number of case studies published in the literature (e.g. Hazelwood & Warren, 2003; Labuschagne, 2006).

Whatever the approach, ideally there are three components to crime linking research—(1) measuring the similarity of crimes (i.e. the behavioural consistency and distinctiveness), (2) predicting linkage status, and (3) testing the accuracy of predictions. Behavioural similarity can be measured in a number of ways including human judgement, similarity coefficients (e.g. Jaccard's coefficient, taxonomic similarity), and spatiotemporal variables (e.g. inter-crime distance and temporal proximity). One of the most common methods for predicting linking status is logistic regression (e.g. Bennell & Canter, 2002; Burrell, 2012; Burrell et al., 2012, 2015; Ellingwood et al., 2013; Markson et al., 2010; Tonkin et al., 2008, 2017; Woodhams & Toye, 2007; Woodhams et al., 2019). Other methods include Discriminant Function Analysis (DFA; e.g. Santtila et al., 2005), Principal Component Analysis (PCA; Santtila et al., 2004), Multiple Correspondence Analysis (MCA; Yokota et al., 2017), Bayesian approaches (e.g. Salo et al., 2012; Tonkin et al., 2017), and Iterative Classification Trees (ICTs; e.g. Tonkin et al., 2012, 2017). Measuring the accuracy of predictions is typically conducted using Receiver Operating Characteristic (ROC). The key statistic in ROC analysis is the Area Under the Curve (AUC). This represents the predictive accuracy of the data that gave rise to the curve. AUC is measured between 0 and 1 where 0.5 represents chance and 1 indicates perfect discrimination. Thus, the higher the AUC, the better the discrimination accuracy. AUCs of 0.5–0.7 are considered moderate, and 0.7–0.9 high (Swets, 1988). In short, ROC allows researchers to assess how good their predictions are compared to the actual linkage status of crimes. Other measures of accuracy include rating the success of suspect prioritisation (e.g. does the suspect appear in the highest ranked offenders generated by a ranking method) or conviction (e.g. in case studies, how many of the cases under discussion resulted in a conviction for the offender). It is worth noting that there is a growing literature utilising machine learning approaches for linking. See Bollé and Casey (2018), Borg and Boldt (2016), and Li and Qi (2019) for examples of such work.

## CRIME LINKAGE OF PERSONAL ROBBERY OFFENCES

This section summarises key findings resulting from Burrell's (2012) PhD research. The findings presented below divided into 4 sets of findings, namely:

1. Ability to link robberies using behaviour

2. The impact of the size of geographical area on linking accuracy
3. The impact of adding more behavioural variables into the analysis
4. The impact of group versus lone offending on linking accuracy.

Note this structure does not match the presentation of the findings exactly as they appear in the thesis; instead, they have been re-structured to streamline presentation and assist the reader to see the key outcomes as identified by the research. Findings 1–3 are directly from the PhD (though note parts of Findings 1–2 are published in Burrell et al., 2012). Findings 4 are from the PhD plus Burrell et al. (2015) which expanded on the original thesis work.

## *Method*

*Samples*
Burrell's (2012) research was conducted using data from two UK police forces—West Midlands Police and Northamptonshire Police. The sample for West Midlands comprised 554 solved offences for 277 offenders (reported between 1 April 2007 and 30 September 2008). The offenders were aged between 11 and 45 years with an average age of 19 at the time of their offence. The majority of offenders ($n = 258$, 93%) were male, and 19 (7%) were female. Over half of the offenders ($n = 138$) were recorded as being from a Black background. Just under 30% were White ($n = 78$), and 15% ($n = 42$) were Asian. Less than 1% ($n = 2$) were from a mixed or other minority ethnic background. Ethnicity was unknown in 6% ($n = 17$) of cases. The sample from Northamptonshire contained 166 offences committed by 83 offenders (reported between 1 January 2005 and 31 December 2007). The offenders were aged between 10 and 44 years with an average age of 18 years at the time of their offence. Seventy-seven offenders were male, and five were female (the gender was unknown for one offender). Over 70% ($n = 58$) of the offenders were recorded as being White (including four females), 13 were Black, and 12 (including 1 female) were of mixed heritage.

*Data Coding*
A text variable was available within the police records (called modus operandi) which outlined a description of how the offence was committed. Content analyses of these descriptions were conducted and a checklist of behaviour variables created. These behaviours were coded

dichotomously (with 1 denoting the presence of a behaviour and 0 the absence of a behaviour) in line with recommendations from the literature (e.g. Canter and Heritage (1990) who stated more complex coding methods are difficult to apply to police recorded crime data). These behaviours were combined with other information from the crime records (e.g. time of day, property stolen) to form a final checklist of behaviours. Behaviours were combined into domains representing themes in the data (namely target selection, control, approach, and property). Inter-crime distance (in metres) and temporal proximity (in days) were also included. A total of 52 behaviours were identified and matched across both police forces. These were used for the initial analysis on the ability to link robberies (findings 1) and if the size of the geographical area impacted accuracy (findings 2). These variables (except approach behaviours) were also used in the analysis to determine if group versus lone offending impacts on predictive accuracy (findings 4). There was additional detail in West Midlands Police data allowing for an extra 26 behaviours to be included in an analysis determine if adding more behaviours boosted predictive accuracy (findings 3). Table 5.1 shows the list of behaviours used and prevalence for both police forces.

A combined domain—comprising target selection, control, approach, and property—and optimal models are also included in Findings 1–3.

*Procedures*

Burrell uses the pairwise approach measuring similarity using Jaccard's coefficients, inter-crime distances, and temporal proximity. Datasets were created comprising of the following in each police force area: (1) linked (pairs of offences committed by the same person), (2) unlinked1 (random pairing up of offences in the dataset using the RAND() function in Excel), and (3) unlinked2 (random pairing up of offences in the dataset using RAND() but controlling for borough/Basic Command Unit (BCU)). Median scores for each dataset are included in Table 5.2.

The unlinked2 datasets were generated to allow further comparison with the associated linked samples. The totally random nature of allocating offences in the unlinked1 datasets means that a single offence could be matched with an unrelated crime located anywhere in the police force area. The police force areas are geographically large—West Midlands is 348 square miles and Northamptonshire is 913 square miles (Office for National Statistics, 2004), and so there is a high likelihood of unlinked

Table 5.1  Checklist of behaviours

| Behavioural domain | Offence behaviours | West Midlands (out of 554 cases) N | % | Northamptonshire (out of 166 cases) N | % |
|---|---|---|---|---|---|
| Target selection | Monday | 89 | 16.1 | 39 | 23.5 |
| | Tuesday | 90 | 16.2 | 22 | 13.3 |
| | Wednesday | 76 | 13.7 | 22 | 13.3 |
| | Thursday | 76 | 13.7 | 23 | 13.9 |
| | Friday | 72 | 13.0 | 24 | 14.5 |
| | Saturday | 75 | 13.5 | 25 | 15.1 |
| | Sunday | 76 | 13.7 | 11 | 6.6 |
| | 22:00 to 01:59 | 91 | 16.4 | 34 | 20.5 |
| | 02:00 to 05:59 | 16 | 2.9 | 5 | 3.0 |
| | 06:00 to 09:59 | 14 | 2.5 | 5 | 3.0 |
| | 10:00 to 13:59 | 76 | 13.7 | 22 | 13.3 |
| | 14:00 to 17:59 | 207 | 37.4 | 46 | 27.7 |
| | 18:00 t0 21:59 | 150 | 27.1 | 54 | 32.5 |
| | Known offender | 106 | 19.1 | 41 | 24.7 |
| | Unknown offender | 226 | 40.8 | 64 | 38.6 |
| | Victim at cashpoint/bank | 8 | 1.4 | 2 | 1.2 |
| | Road* | 291 | 52.5 | [not available/present] | |
| | Private dwelling* | 40 | 7.2 | | |
| | Shops* | 13 | 2.3 | | |
| | Public buildings* | 9 | 1.6 | | |
| | Park/garden* | 64 | 11.6 | | |
| | Bus/bus stop* | 58 | 10.5 | | |
| | Car park* | 18 | 3.2 | | |
| | Public footpath* | 70 | 12.6 | | |
| | Miscellaneous location* | 10 | 1.8 | | |
| Control | Weapon used | 228 | 41.2 | 60 | 36.1 |
| | Knife | 160 | 28.9 | 21 | 12.7 |
| | Firearm | 16 | 2.9 | 4 | 2.4 |
| | Weapon other | 20 | 3.6 | 11 | 6.6 |
| | Knuckleduster* | 8 | 1.4 | [not available/present] | |
| | Cost/baton* | 10 | 1.8 | | |
| | Bottle/glass* | 6 | 1.1 | | |

(continued)

**Table 5.1** (continued)

| Behavioural domain | Offence behaviours | West Midlands (out of 554 cases) N | % | Northamptonshire (out of 166 cases) N | % |
|---|---|---|---|---|---|
| | Iron bar/blunt instrument* | 11 | 2.0 | | |
| | Group of offenders versus group of victims | 137 | 24.7 | 31 | 18.7 |
| | Group of offenders versus lone victim | 240 | 43.3 | 72 | 43.4 |
| | Lone offender versus group of victims | 45 | 8.1 | 9 | 5.4 |
| | Lone offender versus lone victim | 132 | 23.8 | 47 | 28.3 |
| | Offender(s) searches victim(s) property | 172 | 31.0 | 24 | 14.5 |
| | Violence—physical assault | 196 | 35.4 | 55 | 33.1 |
| | Weapon threatened | 183 | 33.0 | 36 | 21.7 |
| | Weapon shown/seen | 168 | 30.3 | 29 | 17.5 |
| | Offender requests property | 116 | 20.9 | 32 | 19.3 |
| | Offender demands property | 172 | 31.0 | 54 | 32.5 |
| | Offender(s) snatch/grab property* | 112 | 20.2 | [not available/present] | |
| | Verbal threat* | 153 | 27.6 | | |
| | Victim resists—met with threat | 47 | 8.5 | 9 | 5.4 |
| | Victim resists—met with violence* | 54 | 9.7 | [not available/present] | |
| Property | Cash | 150 | 27.1 | 39 | 23.5 |
| | Mobile phone | 250 | 45.1 | 51 | 30.7 |
| | Cards | 44 | 7.9 | 8 | 4.8 |
| | Jewellery/watch | 39 | 7.0 | 5 | 3.0 |
| | Wallet/purse | 47 | 8.5 | 11 | 6.6 |
| | Keys | 33 | 6.0 | 6 | 3.6 |
| | Documents | 28 | 5.1 | 8 | 4.8 |
| | Luggage | 36 | 6.5 | 6 | 3.6 |
| | MP3 player | 15 | 2.7 | 7 | 4.2 |

(continued)

**Table 5.1** (continued)

| Behavioural domain | Offence behaviours | West Midlands (out of 554 cases) N | % | Northamptonshire (out of 166 cases) N | % |
|---|---|---|---|---|---|
| | Clothing/footwear | 25 | 4.5 | 7 | 4.2 |
| | Food | 6 | 1.1 | 3 | 1.8 |
| | Cigarettes | 10 | 1.8 | 4 | 2.4 |
| | Pedal cycle | 18 | 3.2 | 14 | 8.4 |
| | Phone (other)* | 6 | 1.1 | [not available/present] | |
| | Car* | 44 | 7.9 | | |
| | Vehicle (other)* | 11 | 2.0 | | |
| | Audio/video equipment* | 25 | 4.5 | | |
| | Computing products* | 13 | 2.3 | | |
| | Fixtures/furnishings* | 7 | 1.3 | | |
| | Property (other)* | 34 | 6.1 | | |
| | Miscellaneous property | 10 | 1.8 | 13 | 7.8 |
| | Property returned | 21 | 3.8 | 3 | 1.8 |
| | Property discarded* | 6 | 1.1 | [not available/present] | |
| Approach | Dupe | 12 | 2.2 | 3 | 1.8 |
| | Carjacking | 17 | 3.1 | 4 | 2.4 |
| | Offender breaks into property | 16 | 2.9 | 6 | 3.6 |
| | Approach from behind | 29 | 5.2 | 7 | 4.2 |
| | Distraction* | 73 | 13.2 | [not available/present] | |
| | Blitz* | 30 | 5.4 | | |
| Inter-crime distance | Inter-crime distance (metres) | | | | |
| Temporal proximity | Temporal proximity (days) | | | | |
| Total | 52 (Findings 1 and 2) | | | | |
| | 78 (Findings 3—extra behaviours denoted with*) | | | | |
| | 48 (Findings 4, as per Findings 1 and 2 but not using approach domain) | | | | |

pairs being located far apart. Further examination of the data revealed that the two offences within linked pairs tended to occur in the same borough/BCU (82% in Northamptonshire and 77% in West Midlands) whereas the two offences within unlinked1 pairs typically occurred in different boroughs/BCUs (75% in Northamptonshire and 95% in West

**Table 5.2** Median scores for behaviours

| Behavioural domain | West Midlands | | | Northamptonshire | | |
|---|---|---|---|---|---|---|
| | Linked | Unlinked1 | Unlinked2 | Linked | Unlinked1 | Unlinked2 |
| Inter-crime distance | 608.59 | 10,356.45 | 2,208.79 | 803.6 | 12,989.8 | 2,313.5 |
| Temporal proximity | 1 | 150 | 137 | 36 | 292 | 144 |
| Target selection | 0.500 | 0.000 | 0.000 | 0.250 | 0.000 | 0.000 |
| Control | 0.333 | 0.143 | 0.143 | 0.250 | 0.167 | 0.125 |
| Property | 0.000 | 0.000 | 0.000 | 0.000 | 0.000 | 0.000 |
| Approach | 0.000 | 0.000 | 0.000 | 0.000 | 0.000 | 0.000 |
| Combined | 0.333 | 0.133 | 0.133 | 0.214 | 0.143 | 0.091 |

Midlands). This difference between the samples of linked and unlinked1 pairs could introduce bias into the analysis, potentially inflating the predictive ability of inter-crime distance and so the unlinked2 sample was created to further explore this. The impact of pushing unlinked pairs closer together geographically is reported under Findings 2 below.

Mann-Whitney U tests were used to determine if there were statistically significant differences between linked and unlinked pairs of offences (with effect sizes reported using $r$). Logistic regression was used to predict linkage status (i.e. linked or unlinked and accuracy testing using ROC (see Burrell, 2012 for more details)). Assumption testing was conducted throughout. Split-half validation was used with experimental samples that had been used to build predictive models and test samples to test predictive models (mirroring the approach used by other researchers—e.g. Bennell & Canter, 2002; Ellingwood et al., 2013) (see Burrell, 2012 for details). For ease and brevity, only the predictive accuracy of regression models and AUCs for the ROC analyses are reported in this chapter. These provide a good summary of findings as they identify which behaviours are most useful for linking and their discrimination accuracy.

### *Findings 1—Ability to Link Robberies Using Behaviour*

The same analysis (regression and ROC) was conducted on identical variables ($n = 52$) in Northamptonshire and the West Midlands. The results revealed that it is possible to predict linkage status (i.e. linked or unlinked) on the basis of behaviour. The analysis revealed that optimal models performed best overall (see Tables 5.3 and 5.4)—these comprised

**Table 5.3** Predictive accuracy of regression models

| | Target selection | Control | Property | Approach | Combined | Inter crime distance | Temporal proximity | Optimal |
|---|---|---|---|---|---|---|---|---|
| West Midlands - Random | 50.0 | 50.0 | 50.0 | 50.0 | 50.0 | 50.0 | 50.0 | 50.0 |
| West Midlands - Unlinked1 | 69.6 | 67.4 | 52.5 | 52.2 | 70.7 | 82.1 | 74.6 | 83.2 |
| Northampton - Random | 50.0 | 50.0 | 50.0 | 50.0 | 50.0 | 50.6 | 50.0 | 50.0 |
| Northamptonshire - Unlinked1 | 65.5 | 56.0 | 56.0 | 51.2 | 63.1 | 81.9 | 66.7 | 83.1 |

**Table 5.4** Discrimination accuracy (linked versus unlinked1 samples)

| Model | AUC (SE) West Midlands | Northamptonshire |
|---|---|---|
| Target selection | 0.777 (0.028)* | 0.640 (0.061)* |
| Control | 0.715 (0.031)* | 0.563 (0.064) |
| Property | 0.581 (0.034)* | 0.448 (0.064) |
| Approach | 0.529 (0.035) | 0.512 (0.064) |
| Combined | 0.805 (0.026)* | 0.635 (0.062)* |
| Inter-crime distance | 0.943 (0.015)* | 0.918 (0.028)* |
| Temporal proximity | 0.868 (0.023)* | 0.829 (0.045)* |
| Optimal | 0.910 (0.018)* | 0.904 (0.033)* |

Note AUC, area under the curve; SE, standard error. An AUC value of 0.5 is non-informative, a value of 0.50–0.70 is low, 0.70–0.90 is moderate, and 0.90–1.00 is high (Swets, 1988) *$p < 0.05$

of target selection, control, inter-crime distance, and temporal proximity in the West Midlands, and target selection and inter-crime distance in Northamptonshire.

Inter-crime distance is the most useful individual factor that can be used to predict linkage status (improving predictive ability over 30% better than chance and achieving an AUC of over 0.9). In short, the closer two offences are, the more likely they are to be linked. Temporal proximity, target selection, and control were all identified as useful linkage factors. There were differences in when and where these individual domains were the most useful (e.g. target selection and control had higher levels of predictive accuracy in West Midlands), but evidence was found for the assumptions in relation to all three across both areas.

It is not surprising that temporal proximity emerged as a useful linkage factor given that the two most recent offences were chosen for each offender to make the linked pair whereas the timeframes were not controlled for in the formation of unlinked pairs. More research which controls for temporal proximity would be useful to shed more light on how reliable this domain is. If evidence is found in favour of temporal proximity as a strong linking factor, this would be useful to analysts because limiting the timeframe for a search would reduce the number of cases under examination. Furthermore, even though analysts already use how close offences are in time and space to make linkage decisions (Burrell & Bull, 2011), it is important to determine whether the evidential base for this is sound.

The target selection domain largely consisted of variables about when offences occurred. There are several reasons why these times of day/days of week might be consistent for an offender. Firstly, from a practical perspective, there may only be particular days or times of day that the offender is available to rob people. Similarly, there are times of day that are more likely to present opportunities to commit robbery (e.g. when there are a lot of people around). With reference to control, the positive results are unsurprising. There is prior evidence available that many robbers develop a consistent method of committing their offences (Deakin et al., 2007) which will include means of controlling victims. Furthermore, people base their actions on previous experience (Harbers et al., 2012; Juliusson et al., 2005) and so if an offender finds an effective method of controlling victim(s), it is likely that he/she will continue to use this method (and therefore display behavioural consistency) in later offences.

The analysis revealed property stolen during the offence is not useful for linkage. This domain performed close to chance in both police force areas. These results are not surprising for several reasons. Firstly, many personal robberies do not actually result in the theft of property with no property recorded as stolen in 22% of the personal robberies in the West Midlands sample (122 out of 554 offences) and 33% of the personal robberies in the Northamptonshire sample (54 out of 166 offences). Furthermore, where property is stolen, these are typically limited to relatively few property types, notably cash and mobile phones (Smith,

2003). It is no coincidence that cash and mobile phones were stolen far more often than any other property type in both Northamptonshire and the West Midlands with cash stolen in 23% of offences (39 out of 166 offences) in Northamptonshire and in 27% of offences (150 out of 554 offences) in the West Midlands. Mobile phones were stolen in between 31% (Northamptonshire) and 45% (West Midlands) of cases. These studies suggest that what is stolen should not be used to make linkage decisions. There may be exceptions where something very distinctive is being targeted (e.g. a particular brand of trainers), but this research indicates property is unlikely to be a useful linkage factor in most cases of personal robbery.

Approach was identified as a poor predictor of linkage status. There are a number of potential reasons why this domain performed so poorly. Firstly, taking the theoretical assumptions into account, it could be that there are only a finite number of approaches used by personal robbers and so the way in which the offender approaches the victim(s) is not distinctive enough. Alternatively, personal robbers might use a variety of approaches depending on circumstances and may not be consistent in their approach behaviour. It is also possible that these results could be due to the low number of behaviours included in the approach domain. Approach was difficult to code due to the absence of information within the modus operandi field about how the offender(s) approached the victim(s), perhaps indicating that information about approach is not routinely collected, recorded, and/or input into crime databases. The knock-on effect of this is that approach behaviours were only recorded for some offences. Indeed, examination of the raw data revealed that information about approach could only be coded for 42% of offences (70 out of 166) in the Northamptonshire sample, and just 32% of the offences (177 out of 554) in the West Midlands. It is possible that sourcing information on the approach for all cases would boost the predictive ability of the approach domain.

The combined domain—which comprised target selection, control, approach, and property—performed better than any of these domains did individually. In West Midlands, this combination did improve overall predictive accuracy (AUC = 0.805) but there was no such benefit in Northamptonshire where the combined domain performed on par with the target selection domain alone (AUCs were 0.635 and 0.640 respectively). Furthermore, neither performed better than the optimal models. Overall, this research has indicated that combining behaviours can boost discrimination accuracy. However, it is important not to just include all behaviours as this will not necessarily work. Furthermore, this research indicates that the combinations of behaviours that are the most useful for linkage might vary depending on where you are working.

### Findings 2—The Impact of the Size of Geographical Area on Linking Accuracy

Due to concerns that the utility of inter-crime distance was being inflated due to the way the unlinked1 sample was generated, a second unlinked sample—which controlled for geography—was compared to the linked sample. Table 5.5 shows the predictive accuracy of the regression models comparing the similarity of linked pairs to unlinked2 pairs of offences (numbers from Table 5.3 are included for easy comparison—new findings are shaded in grey). Table 5.6 shows the discrimination accuracy (again figures from Findings 1 are included for context).

It is clear that the utility of inter-crime distance as a linking factor diminishes when geographical constraints are placed on the data. This is not surprising given the method for generating unlinked2 samples forced the offences in the unlinked pairs closer together. The impact was particularly stark in the West Midlands. This is likely due to how the police forces are structured—at the time the research was conducted, Northamptonshire was 913 square miles and comprised of 6 boroughs. In contrast, West Midlands was 348 square miles and split into 21 Basic Command Units (ranging in size from three square miles to 69 square miles). Thus, the offences were pushed closer together by the formation of unlinked2 samples in West Midlands compared to Northamptonshire. Overall, these findings suggest that the effectiveness of inter-crime distance might be over-estimated in existing research (depending on how they have generated their unlinked samples). However, it is likely inter-crime distance will still be useful as a means of sifting through large volumes of data to reduce the number of cases considered in detail when conducting crime linkage (e.g. limiting a search for linked offences to a local area).

The predictive accuracy of other domains—target selection, control, approach, property, combined, temporal proximity—does not change much in the West Midlands. The optimal model is impacted, likely because it no longer includes inter-crime distance (this is replaced by property in this optimal model). Predictive accuracy is more impacted in Northamptonshire, with some AUCs increasing (target selection, control,

**Table 5.5** Predictive accuracy of regression models controlling for area

| Police force area | Model | Target selection | Control | Property | Approach | Combined | Inter crime distance | Temporal proximity | Optimal |
|---|---|---|---|---|---|---|---|---|---|
| West Midlands | Random | 50.0 | 50.0 | 50.0 | 50.0 | 50.0 | 50.0 | 50.0 | 50.0 |
| | Unlinked1 | 69.6 | 67.4 | 52.5 | 52.2 | 70.7 | 82.1 | 74.6 | 83.2 |
| | Random | 50.4 | 50.4 | 50.4 | 50.4 | 50.4 | 50.2 | 50.4 | 50.2 |
| | Unlinked2 | 67.9 | 69.3 | 54.0 | 51.8 | 72.3 | 35.2 | 73.7 | 79.9 |
| Northamptonshire | Random | 50.0 | 50.0 | 50.0 | 50.0 | 50.0 | 50.6 | 50.0 | 50.0 |
| | Unlinked1 | 65.5 | 56.0 | 56.0 | 51.2 | 63.1 | 81.9 | 66.7 | 83.1 |
| | Random | 50.6 | 50.6 | 50.6 | 50.6 | 50.6 | 50.6 | 50.6 | 50.6 |
| | Unlinked2 | 67.5 | 54.2 | 55.4 | 50.6 | 62.7 | 57.8 | 51.8 | 68.7 |

**Table 5.6** Discrimination accuracy (linked versus unlinked1 and linked versus unlinked2 analyses)

| Model | AUC (SE) | | | |
|---|---|---|---|---|
| | West Midlands | | Northamptonshire | |
| | Unlinked1 | Unlinked2 | Unlinked1 | Unlinked2 |
| Target selection | 0.777 (0.028)* | 0.776 (0.028)* | 0.640 (0.061)* | 0.691 (0.059)* |
| Control | 0.715 (0.031)* | 0.731 (0.030)* | 0.563 (0.064) | 0.657 (0.061)* |
| Property | 0.581 (0.034)* | 0.591 (0.34)* | 0.448 (0.064) | 0.451 (0.064) |
| Approach | 0.529 (0.035) | 0.529 (0.035) | 0.512 (0.064) | 0.512 (0.065) |
| Combined | 0.805 (0.026)* | 0.819 (0.025)* | 0.635 (0.062)* | 0.708 (0.058)* |
| Inter-crime distance | 0.943 (0.015)* | 0.228 (0.029)* | 0.918 (0.028)* | 0.750 (0.055)* |
| Temporal proximity | 0.868 (0.023)* | 0.844 (0.024)* | 0.829 (0.045)* | 0.717 (0.059)* |
| Optimal | 0.910 (0.018)* | 0.846 (0.024)* | 0.904 (0.033)* | 0.782 (0.050)* |

*Note* AUC, area under the curve; SE, standard error. An AUC value of 0.5 is non-informative, a value of 0.50–0.70 is low, 0.70–0.90 is moderate, and 0.90–1.00 is high (Swets, 1988) *$p < 0.05$ (comparing unlinked samples to their corresponding linked samples)

property, combined) and others decreasing (temporal proximity and optimal). Again, the optimal model is likely affected by the diminishing value of inter-crime distance. This time inter-crime distance remains part of the optimal model but the optimal model explained less of the variance compared to the results reported in Findings 1 (31% compared to 69%, see p113 of Burrell, 2012).

There is a drop in performance for temporal proximity in Northamptonshire. Further exploration revealed offences were clustered by date of offence within borough in Northamptonshire which impacted on the effectiveness of the domain. The date of offence was more evenly distributed in the West Midlands data and so the performance of temporal proximity remained stable. Thus, the analysis reveals how easy it is for domain performance to be affected by the uneven distribution of data. This is relevant to all crime linkage researchers, not just those working on personal robbery.

### *Findings 3—The Impact of Adding More Behavioural Variables into the Analysis*

This section focused on determining whether including some additional information in the behavioural domains enhanced their performance in discriminating between linked and unlinked1 crime pairs. It compares the results of analyses using 52 variables to analyses using 78 variables (both conducted in the West Midlands only). See Tables 5.7 and 5.8.

The results indicated that domain performance was broadly unaffected by adding in new variables. Burrell (2012) also tested this with the unlinked2 sample with similar results (i.e. not much change in AUCs between 52 and 78 variables). This is a positive finding; in that it highlights that it is not necessary to include all available information in the search for linked cases. This offers potential to reduce the amount of time needed to source and code information for crime linkage. Further research may be able to reduce the number of behaviours within domains without diluting performance (streamlining the behaviours included if you will).

### *Findings 4—The Impact of Group Versus Lone Offending on Linking Accuracy*

As outlined in Chapter 4, group offending is common in personal robbery. Burrell et al. (2015) tested the impact of group offending on behavioural similarity in serial robbery (again this is part of Burrell's [2012] PhD work but with some additional analyses). The key findings from Burrell et al. (2015) are summarised here.

The linked samples (as outlined above) were utilised for this analysis with an additional variable for the group/lone status of the offences included. West Midlands Police and Northamptonshire Police both recorded the number of defendants associated with offences. This was combined with content analysis of the modus operandi information to identify if each offence was committed by a lone offender or a group (2 or more offenders). In four cases in Northamptonshire there was insufficient information to determine whether the offence was committed by a group or lone offender. The three (known) offenders associated with these cases were therefore removed from the analysis, reducing the number of linked pairs available for analysis from 83 to 80. Unlinked1 datasets (with the one for Northamptonshire reduced to 80 unlinked pairs) were used in the ROC analysis.

The ratio of group versus lone offences was similar across the two police force areas: 65 to 35 per cent in Northamptonshire (104 group and 56 lone out of 160 offences) and 68 to 32 per cent in West Midlands (337 group and 177 lone out of 554 offences). Crime pairs were split into the three categories for analysis: (1) crime pairs where the offender committed

**Table 5.7** Predictive accuracy (adding more variables)

|  |  | Target selection | Control | Property | Approach | Combined | Inter-crime distance | Temporal proximity | Optimal |
|---|---|---|---|---|---|---|---|---|---|
| 52 variables | Random | 50.0 | 50.0 | 50.0 | 50.0 | 50.0 | 50.0 | 50.0 | 50.0 |
|  | Model | 69.6 | 67.4 | 52.5 | 52.2 | 70.7 | 82.1 | 74.6 | 83.2 |
| 78 variables | Random | 50.0 | 50.0 | 50.0 | 50.0 | 50.0 | 50.0 | 50.0 | 50.0 |
|  | Model | 69.9 | 67.4 | 53.3 | 54.3 | 73.2 | 82.1 | 74.6 | 83.6 |

*Note* Inter-crime distance and Temporal proximity were unchanged by adding variables but are included in the table as they form part of the optimal models

**Table 5.8** Discrimination accuracy (adding more variables)

| Model | AUC (SE) 52 variables | AUC (SE) 78 variables |
|---|---|---|
| Target selection | 0.777 (0.028)* | 0.783 (0.028)* |
| Control | 0.715 (0.031)* | 0.717 (0.031)* |
| Property | 0.581 (0.034)* | 0.592 (0.034)* |
| Approach | 0.529 (0.035) | 0.557 (0.034) |
| Combined | 0.805 (0.026)* | 0.817 (0.025)* |
| Optimal | 0.910 (0.018)* | 0.902 (0.019)* |

*Note* AUC, area under the curve; SE, standard error. An AUC value of 0.5 is non-informative, a value of 0.50–0.70 is low, 0.70–0.90 is moderate, and 0.90–1.00 is high (Swets, 1988) *$p < 0.05$

both offences as part of a group (labelled GG), (2) crime pairs where both offences were committed by the same lone offender (labelled LL) and (3) crime pairs where the offender committed one offence as a part of a group and one alone (labelled GL). See Table 5.9 for a breakdown.

Inter-crime distances, temporal proximities, and Jaccard's coefficients for behavioural domains (this time just target selection, control, and property) were compared between GG, LL, and GL linked pairs. Kruskal-Wallis tests were used to determine if there were statistically significant differences between GG, LL, and GL pairs for each of the behavioural domains. There were no statistically significant differences between GG or LL pairs for any behaviour. This indicates that pairs of group offences display similar levels of behavioural consistency as pairs of lone offences which is important as it suggests it is possible to link group offences based on behaviour.

**Table 5.9** Frequency of GG, LL, and GL pairs

| Pair consists of | Northamptonshire Linked (%) | Northamptonshire Unlinked (%) | West Midlands Linked (%) | West Midlands Unlinked (%) |
|---|---|---|---|---|
| Two group offences (GG) | 38 (47.5) | 34 (42.5) | 165 (59.6) | 130 (46.9) |
| Two Lone offences (LL) | 14 (17.5) | 10 (12.5) | 65 (23.5) | 30 (10.8) |
| One group/one lone offence (GL) | 28 (35.0) | 36.0 (45.0) | 47 (17.0) | 117 (42.2) |
| Total pairs | 80 (100) | 80 (100) | 277 (100) | 277 (100) |

However, there were crucial differences in control revealed by this analysis. Firstly, the behavioural similarity of linked GL pairs was low for the control domain, with median scores of just 0.143 in the West Midlands and 0.000 in Northamptonshire. Furthermore, the Kruskal–Wallis found a significant difference for control (Northamptonshire – $\chi^2(2) = 21.384$; $p < 0.001$; West Midlands – $\chi^2(2) = 34.043$; $p < 0.001$). Post-hoc tests (Mann-Whitney U with Bonferroni correction) revealed this difference to be between GL and GG (Northamptonshire – $p < 0.001$; $r = 0.43$; West Midlands – $p < 0.001$; $r = 0.39$) and between GL and LL (Northamptonshire $p < 0.001$; $r = 0.69$; West Midlands – $p < 0.001$; $r = 0.46$). This means there are lower levels of behavioural consistency for GL pairs compared to GG or LL pairs. This is not surprising given that groups and lone offenders utilise violence and weapons differently (Burrell et al., 2015). This means that control behaviours cannot be used to link group offences to lone offences committed by the same offender.

The Kruskal-Wallis test also revealed a significant difference in relation to temporal proximity in Northamptonshire ($\chi^2(2) = 6.304$; $p = 0.043$) with showing this difference was between GL and GG pairs ($p = 0.014$; $r = 0.30$). This could be due to variations in decision-making—e.g. offenders are being more selective about when they commit an offence when they are alone. However, this finding is more likely to be an artefact of the data distribution. Re-examination of the raw data revealed that date of offence was unevenly distributed with offences in some boroughs clustered towards the start of the timeframe, and others in different boroughs clustered towards the end. It is, therefore, inappropriate to make recommendations based on this finding. The analysis also revealed a difference for target selection in West Midlands ($\chi^2(2) = 6.342$; $p = 0.042$) with a difference between GL and LL albeit with a small effect size ($p = 0.017$; $r = 0.16$). This could be due to differences in decision-making when working alone compared to when offending in a group. More research is needed to unpick this.

ROC was used to examine whether it was possible to distinguish between linked and unlinked pairs of offences whilst controlling for group/lone status. The most useful behaviours were identified as inter-crime distance and temporal proximity for all kinds of pairs (see Table 5.10). There are some differences between police force areas for discrimination accuracy with AUCs often higher in West Midlands compared to Northamptonshire (e.g. target selection). There are also differences across GG, LL, and GL comparisons with many domains performing

Table 5.10 Discrimination accuracy for GG, LL, and GL pairs

| Sample | Behavioural domain | AUC (SE)—Northamptonshire | AUC (SE)—West Midlands |
| --- | --- | --- | --- |
| Linked GG pairs versus unlinked1 GG pairs | Inter-crime distance | 0.940 (0.025)* | 0.944 (0.013)* |
| | Temporal proximity | 0.830 (0.047)* | 0.860 (0.022)* |
| | Target selection | 0.683 (0.063)* | 0.765 (0.027)* |
| | Control | 0.477 (0.069) | 0.699 (0.030)* |
| | Property | 0.478 (0.069) | 0.534 (0.034) |
| Linked LL pairs versus unlinked1 LL pairs | Inter-crime distance | 0.857 (0.085)* | 0.927 (0.030)* |
| | Temporal proximity | 0.850 (0.082)* | 0.838 (0.040)* |
| | Target selection | 0.646 (0.112) | 0.764 (0.050)* |
| | Control | 0.775 (0.096)* | 0.719 (0.054)* |
| | Property | 0.607 (0.116) | 0.613 (0.058) |
| Linked GL pairs versus unlinked1 GL pairs | Inter-crime distance | 0.895 (0.042)* | 0.923 (0.024)* |
| | Temporal proximity | 0.701 (0.070)* | 0.884 (0.031)* |
| | Target selection | 0.585 (0.073) | 0.697 (0.051)* |
| | Control | 0.579 (0.073) | 0.588 (0.052) |
| | Property | 0.482 (0.073) | 0.547 (0.051) |

slightly better for GG and LL comparisons compared to GL. Again, the differences between lone and group offending could explain some of these differences. The most interesting domain is control which generally performs better in the West Midlands compared to Northamptonshire and LL samples (indicating it could be used to link lone offences committed by the same offender to each other). Control does not have good discrimination accuracy in GG groups in Northamptonshire. Although better in West Midlands, the AUC still does not reach 0.7. In GL pairs, control is not performing much above chance. Altogether, these results indicate that control is an unreliable linking factor for group offending, particularly when trying to link group offences to lone offences committed by the same offender.

Overall, Findings 4 identify some limitations when attempting to link robberies the offender had committed alone to ones they had committed as part of a group. However, there were still opportunities to link depending on which behaviour was used (Burrell et al., 2015). These findings demonstrate the value of continued work to identify useful linking behaviours.

## LIMITATIONS

There are limitations to this study and the behavioural crime linkage literature more broadly. There are gaps between how linkage is tested in research studies and how the principles are applied in practice; the wider this gap, the less applicable the research might be. Core limitations, and if/how they apply to the research in this chapter, are outlined to provide the reader with an overview of the issues which researchers are facing (and trying to overcome). Much of the prior crime linkage research—including this study—has been conducted using police recorded crime data. The limitations of working with police data are clearly outlined in the literature, including the challenges presented by possible inaccuracies (Tonkin et al., 2008), and the inability to assess the reliability of data coding within police data systems (Bennell & Canter, 2002). Furthermore, it is well reported in the criminology literature that crime under-reporting is a perennial problem (Felson, 2002). With reference to crime linkage, under-reporting results in gaps in data (Ainsworth, 2001) potentially making it more difficult to identify series as some offences in the series might not have been reported to the police.

This research utilised solved offences. This raises concerns as, not only is this unrepresentative of crime linkage in an applied setting (Tonkin, et al., 2012), but it is also possible that the reason cases were solved is because they were behaviourally similar and/or geographically and temporally proximal (Bennell & Jones, 2005). Thus, using solved offences could inflate the similarity scores or artificially reduce the geographical and temporal distances of linked offences compared to unsolved serial crimes. This research was also limited to serial cases; again, this might skew the data as it could be argued that some offences might be on-offs (i.e. individual offences and not part of a series). Some researchers (e.g. Woodhams & Labuschagne, 2011; Woodhams et al., 2019) have addressed this by including unsolved-but-linked-by-DNA cases in their samples. Positively, the findings indicate that the theoretical assumptions of linkage still hold with these more ecologically valid datasets.

The research discussed in this chapter compared a linked sample to unlinked samples of a comparable size (as the research focused on controlling the size of the area in each phase). In an applied setting, the analyst is looking for series of offences from within all recorded crime. Thus, limiting the sample of unlinked pairs in this way is not reflective of the linkage task and this might have inflated or depressed the value of behavioural domains for linkage. This limitation could be overcome by comparing the linked sample to all possible combinations of unlinked pairs, and that is indeed the approach used in most research (i.e. including all possible pairwise comparisons in the analysis).

Finally, as mentioned earlier in the chapter, researchers are using a wide range of methods to test the assumptions of crime linkage and linkage accuracy. This makes it difficult to compare the relative performance of different approaches and develop reliable recommendations for the police. Tonkin et al. (2017) used ROC to compare the performance of different statistical approaches to linkage (in rape) including regression, iterative classification trees, and Bayesian methods. All models performed well with one Bayesian method achieving an AUC of 0.91. The research concluded that statistical approaches that utilise individual offender behaviours when generating crime linkage predictions may be preferable to approaches that rely on a single summary score of behavioural similarity.

## Future Research

Researchers must continue to build the evidence base for behavioural crime linkage. This includes identifying which behaviours can be used to accurately predict whether crimes are linked. Explorations of different crime types, in different cultures, and with larger, more ecologically valid datasets are needed. Further testing of similarity scores (e.g. Jaccard's) and methods (e.g. regression, ROC, Bayesian approaches) is needed with consideration for how this work could feed into automated systems to support analyst decision-making.

## Conclusion

The findings of the study reported in this chapter indicate it is possible to distinguish between linked and unlinked pairs of personal robbery offences using behaviour, thus indicating behavioural crime linkage is possible on this offence type. Although there were some differences in performance when comparing urban and rural police forces (West Midlands compared to Northamptonshire), when placing geographical constraints on the data (i.e. limiting the area when unlinked pairs could be matched), and when taking group offending into account, the overarching finding is that there is evidence for the underlying assumptions of BCL with personal robbery data. Future research should focus on identifying which behaviours in which contexts are the most useful for linking.

## References

Ainsworth, P. B. (2001). *Offender profiling and crime analysis*. Willan.

Alarid, L. F., Burton, V. S., & Hochstetler, A. L. (2009). Group and solo robberies: Do accomplices shape criminal form? *Journal of Criminal Justice, 37*, 1–9. https://doi.org/10.1016/j.jcrimjus.2008.12.001

Bennell, C., & Canter, D. V. (2002). Linking commercial burglaries by modus operandi: Tests using regression and ROC analysis. *Science & Justice, 42*, 153–164. https://doi.org/10.1016/S1355-0306(02)71820-0

Bennell, C., & Jones, N. J. (2005). Between a ROC and a hard place: A method for linking serial burglaries by modus operandi. *Journal of Investigative Psychology and Offender Profiling, 2*, 23–41. https://doi.org/10.1002/jip.21

Bennell, C., Jones, N. J., & Melnyk, T. (2009). Addressing problems with traditional crime linking methods using receiver operating characteristic analysis. *Legal and Criminological Psychology, 14*, 293–310. https://doi.org/10.1348/135532508X349336

Bollé, T., & Casey, E. (2018). Using computed similarity of distinctive digital traces to evaluate non-obvious links and repetitions in cyber-investigations. *Digital Investigation, 24*, S2–S9. https://doi.org/10.1016/j.diin.2018.01.002

Borg, A., & Boldt, M. (2016). Clustering residential burglaries using modus operandi and spatiotemporal information. *International Journal of Information Technology & Decision Making, 15*(1), 23–42. https://doi.org/10.1142/S0219622015500339

Burrell, A. (2012). *Behavioural case linkage in personal robbery* (PhD thesis). University of Leicester. https://leicester.figshare.com/articles/thesis/Behavioural_Case_Linkage_in_Personal_Robbery/10147652/1

Burrell, A., & Bull, R. (2011). A preliminary examination of crime analysts' views and experiences of Comparative Case Analysis. *International Journal of Police Science and Management, 13*, 2–15. https://doi.org/10.1350/ijps.2011.13.1.212

Burrell, A., Bull, R., & Bond, J. (2012). Linking personal robbery offences using offender behaviour. *Journal of Investigative Psychology and Offender Profiling, 9*(3), 201–222. https://doi.org/10.1002/jip.1365

Burrell, A., Bull, R., Bond, J., & Herrington, G. (2015). Testing the impact of group offending on behavioural similarity in serial robbery. *Psychology, Crime & Law, 21*(6), 551–569. https://doi.org/10.1080/1068316X.2014.999063

Canter, D. (1995). Psychology of offender profiling. In R. Bull & D. Carson (Eds.), *Handbook of psychology in legal contexts* (pp. 343–355). Wiley.

Canter, D., & Heritage, R. (1990). A multivariate model of sexual offences behaviour: Developments in 'offender profiling.' *Journal of Forensic Psychiatry*, 1, 185–212. https://doi.org/10.1080/09585189008408469

Deakin, J., Smithson, H., Spencer, J., & Medina-Ariza, J. (2007). Taxing on the streets: Understanding the methods and process of street robbery. *Crime Prevention and Community Safety*, 9, 52–76. https://doi.org/10.1057/palgrave.cpcs.8150033

Douglas, J. E., & Munn, C. (1992). Violent crime scene analysis: Modus operandi, signature, and staging. *FBI Law Enforcement Bulletin*. http://www.criminalprofiling.ch/violent-crime.html

Ellingwood, H., Mugford, R., Bennell, C., Melnyk, T., & Fritzon, K. (2013). Examining the role of similarity coefficients and the value of behavioural themes in attempts to link serial arson offences. *Journal of Investigative Psychology and Offender Profiling*, 10(1), 1–27. https://doi.org/10.1002/jip.1364

Ewart, B. W., Oatley, G. C., & Burn, K. (2005). Matching crime using burglars' modus operandi: A test of three models. *International Journal of Police Science & Management*, 7, 160–174. https://doi.org/10.1350/ijps.2005.7.3.160

Felson, M. (2002). *Crime and everyday life* (3rd ed.). Sage.

Goodwill, A. M., & Alison, L. J. (2006). The development of a filter model for prioritizing suspects in burglary offences. *Psychology, Crime, & Law*, 12, 395–416. https://doi.org/10.1080/10683160500056945

Grubin, D., Kelly, P., & Brunsdon, C. (2001). *Linking serious sexual assaults through behaviour* (Home Office Research Study 215). Home Office.

Harbers, E., Deslauriers-Varin, N., Beauregard, E., & van der Kemp, J. J. (2012). Testing the behavioural and environmental consistency of serial sex offenders: A signature approach. *Journal of Investigative Psychology and Offender Profiling*. Advance online publication. https://doi.org/10.1002/jip.1368

Hauffe, S., & Porter, L. (2009). An interpersonal comparison of lone and group rape offences. *Psychology, Crime, and Law*, 15, 469–491. https://doi.org/10.1080/10683160802409339

Hazelwood, R. R., & Warren, J. I. (2003). Linkage analysis: Modus operandi, ritual, and signature in serial sexual crime. *Aggression and Violent Behavior*, 8, 587–598. https://doi.org/10.1016/j.avb.2004.02.002

Juliusson, E. Á., Karlsson, N., & Gärling, T. (2005). Weighing the past and future in decision making. *European Journal of Cognitive Psychology*, 17, 561–575. https://doi.org/10.1080/09541440440000159

Keppel, R. D. (1995). Signature murders: A report of several related cases. *Journal of Forensic Science, 40*, 670–674. https://doi.org/10.1002/jip.22

Labuschagne, G. N. (2006). The use of a linkage analysis as evidence in the conviction of the Newcastle serial murderer, South Africa. *Journal of Investigative Psychology and Offender Profiling, 3*, 183–191. https://doi.org/10.1002/jip.51

Labuschagne, G. (2012). The use of a linkage analysis as an investigative tool and evidential material in serial offenses. In K. Borgeson & K. Kuehnle (Eds.), *Serial offenders: Theory and practice* (pp. 187–215). Jones & Bartlett Learning LLC.

Li, Y., & Qi, M. (2019). An approach for understanding offender modus operandi to detect serial robbery crimes. *Journal of Computational Science, 36*, 101024. https://doi.org/10.1016/j.jocs.2019.101024

Markson, L., Woodhams, J., & Bond, J. (2010). Linking serial residential burglary: Comparing the utility of modus operandi behaviours, geographical proximity, and temporal proximity. *Journal of Investigative Psychology & Offender Profiling, 7*, 91–107. https://doi.org/10.1002/jip.120

Office for National Statistics. (2004). *Rural & Urban Area Classification 2004*. http://www.ons.gov.uk/ons/publications/re-reference-tables.html?edition=tcm%3A77-211129

Porter, L. E., & Alison, L. J. (2006a). Behavioural coherence in group robbery: A circumplex model of offender and victim interactions. *Aggressive Behavior, 32*, 330–342. https://doi.org/10.1002/ab.20132

Porter, L. E., & Alison, L. J. (2006b). Examining group rape: A descriptive analysis of offender and victim behaviour. *European Journal of Criminology, 3*, 357–381. https://doi.org/10.1177/1477370806065586

Salfati, C. G., Horning, A. M., Sorochinski, M., & Labuschagne, G. N. (2014). South African serial homicide: Consistency in victim types and crime scene actions across series. *Journal of Investigative Psychology and Offender Profiling, 12*, 83–106. https://doi.org/10.1002/jip.1428

Salo, B., Sirén, J., Corander, J., Zappalà, A., Bosco, D., Mokros, A., & Santtila, P. (2012). Using Bayes' theorem in behavioural crime linking of serial homicide. *Legal and Criminological Psychology, 18*(2), 356–370. https://doi.org/10.1111/j.2044-8333.2011.02043.x

Santtila, P., Fritzon, K., & Tamelander, A. (2004). Linking arson incidents on the basis of crime scene behavior. *Journal of Police and Criminal Psychology, 19*, 1–16. https://doi.org/10.1007/BF02802570

Santtila, P., Junkkila, J., & Sandnabba, N.K. (2005). Behavioural linking of stranger rapes. *Journal of Investigative Psychology and Offender Profiling, 2*, 87–103. https://doi.org/10.1002/jip.26

Smith, J. (2003). *The nature of personal robbery* (Home Office research phase 254). Home Office. http://library.npia.police.uk/docs/hors254.pdf

Sorochinski, M., & Salfati, C. G. (2010). The consistency of inconsistency in serial homicide: Patterns of behavioural change across series. *Journal of Investigative Psychology & Offender Profiling*, 7, 109–136. https://doi.org/10.1002/jip.118

Swets, J. A. (1988). Measuring the accuracy of diagnostic systems. *Science*, 240, 1285–1293. https://doi.org/10.1126/science.3287615

Tilley, N., Smith, J., Finer, S., Erol, R., Charles, C., & Dobby, J. (2004). *Problem solving street crime: Practical lessons from the street crime initiative*. Home Office.

Tjin-A-Tsoi, T. B. P. M. (2013). *Trends, challenges and strategy in the forensic science sector*. Report for the Netherlands Forensic Institute. https://www.forensicinstitute.nl/about_nfi/news/2013/white-paper-on-trends-challenges-and-strategy-in-forensic-science.aspx

Tonkin, M., Grant, T., & Bond, J. W. (2008). To link or not to link: A test of the case linkage principles using serial car theft data. *Journal of Investigative Psychology and Offender Profiling*, 5, 59–77. https://doi.org/10.1002/jip.74

Tonkin, M., Woodhams, J., Bull, R., Bond, J. W., & Santtila, P. (2012). A comparison of logistic regression and classification tree analysis for behavioural case linkage. *Journal of Investigative Psychology and Offender Profiling*, 9, 235–258. https://doi.org/10.1002/jip.1367

Tonkin, M., Pakkanen, T., Sirén, J., Bennell, C., Woodhams, J., Burrell, A., Imre, H., Winter, J. M., Lam, E., ten Brinke, G., Webb, M., Labuschagne, G. N., Ashmore-Hills, L., van der Kemp, J. J., Lipponen, S., Rainbow, L., Salfati, C. G., & Santtila, P. (2017). Using offender crime scene behavior to link stranger sexual assaults: A comparison of three statistical approaches. *Journal of Criminal Justice*, 50, 19–28. https://doi.org/10.1016/j.jcrimjus.2017.04.002

Woodhams, J., & Labuschagne, G. (2011). A test of crime linkage principles with solved and unsolved serial rapes. *Journal of Police and Criminal Psychology*, 27, 85–98. https://doi.org/10.1007/s11896-011-9091-1

Woodhams, J., & Toye, K. (2007). An empirical test of the assumptions of case linkage and offender profiling with serial commercial robberies. *Psychology, Public Policy, and Law*, 13, 59–85. https://doi.org/10.1037/1076-8971.13.1.59

Woodhams, J., Tonkin, M., Burrell, A., Imre, H., Winter, J. M., Lam, E. K. M., ten Brinke, G., Webb, M., Labuschagne, G., Bennell, C., Ashmore-Hills, L., van der Kemp, J., Lipponen, S., Pakkanen, T., Rainbow, L., Salfati, C. C., & Santtila, P. (2019). Linking serial sexual offences: Moving towards an ecologically valid test of the principles of crime linkage XE "crime linkage." *Legal and Criminological Psychology*, 24(1), 123–140. https://doi.org/10.1111/lcrp.12144

Yokota, K., & Watanabe, S. (2002). Computer-based retrieval of suspects using similarity of modus operandi. *International Journal of Police Science & Management, 4*, 5–15.

Yokota, K., Watanabe, K., Wachi, T., Otsuka, Y., Hirama, K., & Fujita, G. (2017). Crime linkage of sex offences in Japan by multiple correspondence analysis. *Journal of Investigative Psychology and Offender Profiling, 14*(2), 109–119. https://doi.org/10.1002/jip.1468

CHAPTER 6

# Profiling Robbery Offenders

**Abstract** This chapter will outline profiling methods—for example, predictive profiling (of offender characteristics) and geographical profiling—and how they could be used in robbery cases. Often used on serial cases (after crime linkage via forensics and/or behaviour—see Chapter 5 for more on Behavioural Crime Linkage), these methods can help the police to prioritise who or what to look for. Relevant theoretical frameworks (e.g. homology, distance decay, domocentricity) will be explained along with a discussion of how these methods might be applied to robbery cases.

**Keywords** Profiling · Serial crimes · Homology · Distance decay · Domocentricity

## INTRODUCTION

Profiling uses offender behaviour to try to identify characteristics of offenders (e.g. age, education level, employment status, where an offender lives/works/socialises). It has become a popular topic for media (Herndon, 2007) which can lead to misconceptions about its nature and use. It is therefore important to understand what profiling is (and is not!) and so this chapter aims to provide a brief introduction to two profiling

© The Author(s), under exclusive license to Springer Nature
Switzerland AG 2022
A. Burrell, *Robbery*,
https://doi.org/10.1007/978-3-030-93173-5_6

techniques and summarise the potential for using these with robbery cases.

## Predictive Profiling

Predictive profiling—otherwise referred to as offender profiling or criminal profiling—is an investigative tool which aims to deduce offender characteristics based on crime scene behaviour (Ainsworth, 2000). In short, it is the process of predicting demographic and social characteristics of a person based on how they commit their offences. The idea of predicting offender characteristics based on behaviour is not new—for example, the coroner in the infamous Jack the Ripper case in London (1888) noted that an abattoir worker would have had the necessary skill to commit the offences (Knight & Watson, 2017). The use of profiling has been popularised in the media through TV programmes and movies (Herndon, 2007) influencing the public perceptions of what profiling is. However, some of these views are not representative of what profiling is here and now in the UK. For example, contrary to popular belief, predictive profiling is not about predicting personality. Although this has been an approach used in the past by profilers, it does not represent the UK approach to profiling (Alison & Rainbow, 2011), where the focus is placed on what would be useful to the investigation rather than psychological insights (Rainbow & Gregory, 2011). Positively, more research into the reliability and utility of profiling gained traction in the 1970s and 1980s, and a much better understanding of the technique has been developed in the last 20 years (Fox & Farrington, 2018).

In the UK, predictive profiling is conducted by Behavioural Investigative Advisors (BIAs) and regulated through ensuring a clear remit, scope, and appropriate expertise of profilers (Rainbow, 2011). When undertaking predictive profiling work, BIAs will strive to identify characteristics of the offender which might offer practical investigative lines of enquiry. For example, whether they are likely to have a police record and for what kinds of offences (Rainbow & Gregory, 2011). They might also work with a Geographical Profiler to try to determine where the offender lives (more on this later in the chapter).

## Theoretical Framework

Predictive profiling hinges on the core assumption of homology—that is, a meaningful relationship exists between offender behaviour and background characteristics (Mokros & Alison, 2002). More specifically, homology assumes offenders who commit crime in a similar way will share similar background characteristics (Alison et al., 2011). It is important to assess the evidence base for homology—without it, the legitimacy of profiling can be questioned (Doan & Snook, 2008). In short, we cannot expect profiling to work in practice if we have no evidence for homology.

Research on the homology assumption often takes the form of testing typologies. Researchers will identify styles of offending based on offence behaviour and look for evidence to indicate that certain types of people (e.g. males, young people) are more likely to fit into one style of offending over another. If this happens, there is evidence for homology.

A second set of assumptions that is useful to consider in predictive profiling is behavioural consistency and behavioural distinctiveness. These are core assumptions of crime linkage (see Chapter 5) and would be relevant to profilers working on serial cases. There is evidence for these assumptions in robbery (see, for example, Burrell et al., 2012). Of particular relevance for profiling is the finding that not all offender behaviours are consistent over time (see Chapter 5 for examples of behaviours which are not consistent across crime series [e.g. property stolen]). This means it is important for the profiler to identify which offence behaviours are the most salient when making predictions about the offender's background characteristics. For example, it has been shown that behaviours which are under the offender's control (e.g. where they offend) are more consistent than behaviours that might arise from the situation (e.g. what is stolen will depend on what the victim is carrying). Focusing on behaviours the offender has more control over should, therefore, provide more insights.

## Profiling Robbery Offenders

Profiling can be a useful investigative tool. However, it is important to remember that the aim of this technique is not about solving a case (Rainbow & Gregory, 2011), it is about supporting police decision making (Rainbow et al., 2011; Rainbow & Gregory, 2011). Perhaps the most obvious way is through suspect prioritisation (i.e. helping to narrow down or rank order suspect lists to try to identify the perpetrator more quickly). There are other potential uses though—for example, identifying search strategies and developing strategies for interviewing suspects. So, can this approach support robbery investigations?

Research for this book has revealed little in the way of research about profiling robbery offenders. Where literature has been found, this often relates to commercial robbery and/or is not based on UK data. An exception is made in this chapter to therefore move away from the tight focus on personal robbery in the UK to open up a wider discussion around profiling robbery offenders.

*Typologies*

Typologies are a means of classifying things, in this instance types of offences/offenders. The most well known is the organised versus disorganised dichotomy (Hazelwood & Douglas, 1980). Organised offenders are described as meticulous individuals who engage in high-level planning against specific targets and demonstrate forensic awareness. By contrast, disorganised offenders behave more chaotically and their behaviour suggests a lack of planning (Kocsis et al., 1998). There are a few typologies of robbery offences in the literature, including specific types suggested for personal robbery. There are some typologies which relate to commercial robbery—these will also be discussed for context and to make comparisons.

There are different ways to develop a typology. Some have been based around level of planning (similar to the organised/disorganised approach). For example, Walsh (1986) classified commercial robbers as either "planners" or "opportunists". Smith (2003) used the approach tactic, suggesting that personal robbery offenders can be classified into one of four themes based on this. These are: (1) Con: the victim is initially distracted by the offender or lulled into a false sense of security; (2) Confrontation: the victim is confronted with a demand for property; (3) Snatch: offender grabs for property that is on display; and (4) Blitz: offender overwhelms the victim with physical violence with no warning.

Goodwill et al. (2012) built on Smith's (2003) work utilising data from 72 robbery offenders to try to classify 28 behavioural variables into these 4 robbery styles. Using multi-dimensional scaling, they demonstrated that the theoretical groupings of behavioural variables did correspond strongly with Smith's (2003) typology. Furthermore, the results indicated the presence of two behavioural facets—level of interaction and level of violence. For example, blitz offences were categorised as low interaction, high violence offences. These facets were developed using the specific crime scene behaviours associated with them (e.g. finding blitz attacks are more aggressive and include multiple acts of violence).

Yapp's (2010) doctoral work is on the profiling of robbery offenders. Through a semi-systematic review of the literature plus empirical studies, he identified two types of robbery offender: the career professional and the amateur anti-social robber. The profiles of these two offender types are perhaps unsurprising—the career professionals were older and more experienced. They were more likely to commit commercial offences and offend in a planned and controlled manner. Their offences were characterised by high levels of interaction and lower levels of violence. In contrast, the amateur anti-social robber is likely to be opportunistic and chaotic in their offending and/or be under the influence of illegal substances. They are more likely to commit offences outside and have previous convictions for offences against people and property. Their offences are characterised by high levels of violence and low levels of interaction. Yapp (2010) identifies characteristics associated with each type of offender. For example, amateurs were typically under 30, had left school early, and had few employable skills. He also notes professionals tended to operate in groups (where planning and assigning roles is more important) and amateurs alone.

Other typologies have incorporated more psychological aspects. For example, Alison et al. (2000) argue that robbers have self-adopted roles and narratives that form part of their everyday functioning. This includes their offending where the capacity to plan (proactive versus reactive) and maintain self-control (impulsive versus rational) is expressed through their offence behaviours. They proposed three robber typologies: Robin's men, Bandits, and Cowboys. Robin's men are professionals (e.g. bank robbers) who are often career criminals. Robin's men carefully plan their offences and are skilled enough to adapt to situations that might arise. Bandits are conceptualised as "outlaws". They also engage in planning behaviour but are less likely to consider how to manage issues that come up during the offence. Their tactics are extremely aggressive and can escalate if they feel they are losing control of the situation. Cowboys are opportunists who often commit crimes recklessly with little planning and may be offending to fund a drug habit. Testing this typology using data from 144 armed robberies, Alison et al. (2000) did find robbery fell into these three broad categories. In addition, they found there were some behaviours which were shared across robbery type—e.g. surprise attack, bringing a weapon, using verbal instructions. These were all actions associated with the start of an offence suggesting that later behaviours would be more useful to distinguish between robbery types.

Planning and impulsivity are also considered by Piotrowski (2011) who argues there are three types of street robbery offenders (1) the rational, (2) the bounded rational, and (3) the irrational. Rational offenders are experienced and plan their offences carefully. They are professionals motivated by material gain. Offenders in this group had committed previous offences, and criminality was a core element of the environments they grew up in. The second group—who display bounded rationality—mostly acted under the influence of alcohol. Some were motivated by a perceived injustice, and peer pressure and street culture were underlying factors. Irrational offenders are impulsive and offences might be described as an "act of stupidity". Piotrowski (2011) describes these offenders as paratelic dominant—i.e. playful, spontaneous, and arousal seeking.

Our understanding of who fits into typologies is further extended by Harding et al. (2019). This study explored the relationship between gangs and robbery through interviews with 42 current and ex-street offenders and found that robbery type was affected by the level of gang organisation. The research produced a typology of gang organisation and street robbery with different offence characteristics evident across young street gangs, criminal gangs, and serious and organised crime groups. The research found that young street gangs centre around recreation but with some delinquency and crime. With regard to robbery, this was typically committed to gain peer approval or build "street capital" (Harding, 2014). Three forms of robbery emerged for this group: (1) opportunistic robbery of criminal peers, (2) street robbery of other young people (e.g. clubbers), and (3) targeting the general public (Harding et al., 2019). Criminal gangs tend to be smaller groups with a few core members. Offending is more targeted (especially of other offenders, e.g. drug dealers) and planned and proceeds are divided between members. Criminal gang members are older, physically more developed, and more emotionally mature than the young street gang members and crime is more central to the group's activities. Offending is more profit driven than for young street gangs who tend to be motivated by the excitement or opportunity to bond with other members of the group. Serious and organised crime groups take robbery even further in terms of profits and planning. Robbery is now a business and criminal activity is well organised and delivered by an experienced team of professionals. Serious and organised crime groups are more risk adverse as limiting risk can help maximise profits. However, they will target other offenders if there is a perceived threat to "business"—that is, robbery can be used to scare rivals. The serious and organised crime groups are also more diverse in their offending, expanding into more complex crime such as fraud (Harding et al., 2019).

*Differences Between Commercial and Personal Robbery*
Research on typologies has identified differences between personal and commercial robbery. Porter and Alison (2006a) use a circumplex model to examine behavioural coherence in group robbery. The circumplex offers two dimensions of behaviour—Submission/Dominance and Cooperation/Hostility—that can be used to examine the interactions between offenders and victims during the offence. The circumplex is not designed to offer a regional-based typology (i.e. clear, distinguishable categories); instead, it offers a way to visualise behaviour as a reflection of the two dimensions. This research found differences between commercial and personal offences that may be useful for profiling purposes (e.g. could indicate different types of offenders commit personal versus commercial robberies). The study found commercial robbery was significantly more likely to use a co-operative interpersonal style of offending. In contrast, personal robberies were characterised by hostility. Other research has also found differences between commercial and personal offences. For example, Alison et al. (2000) report commercial robbers were more likely to wear a disguise, and Porter and Alison (2006a) found commercial robberies were more likely to be surprise attack. Personal robberies have been found to be more violent (Porter & Alison, 2006b), possibly because it has also been found victims are more likely to resist personal robbers (Alison et al., 2000; Porter & Alison, 2006b).

*Challenges Presented by Groups*
It is impossible to ignore the impact of group dynamics on robbery (see Chapter 4) and profiling is no exception. Groups mean that more than one offender is contributing to the behaviour profile of an offence and so members of groups need to behave in a homogenous way if we are going to classify each offence into a typology (Porter & Alison, 2006a). Within group similarity does occur in robbery (Porter & Alison, 2006a) and is often modelled on the behaviour of the leader (Porter & Alison,

2006b). This suggests that it would be possible to classify group offences into typologies.

*Testing the Homology Assumption*
There are few tests of the homology assumption in robbery and, unfortunately, these studies indicate the evidence is weak for homology in robbery. Woodhams and Toye (2007) conducted hierarchical cluster analysis, which identified three behavioural types in a sample of UK commercial robbers. The homology assumption would predict that offenders from different behavioural types would differ in terms of their personal characteristics. However, the offenders did not differ in terms of age, journey-to-crime, ethnicity, or employment status.

Doan and Snook (2008) also found no evidence for the homology assumption in their samples of commercial robbery committed in Canada. They assigned crimes to Alison et al.'s (2000) robbery typology— Cowboys (75%), Bandits (22%), and Robin's men (2%) (1% were identified as mixed) and then tested the associations between these types and a range of offender characteristics for the Cowboys and Bandits groups (Robin's men and mixed were excluded due to small sample sizes). They examined variables including age, psychiatric history, and criminal record. They found some statistically significant associations between robbery type and characteristics. Specifically, Bandits were more likely to have been to prison and to have been arrested (for weapons, violent behaviour, and robbery offences). However, effect sizes were small and no associations were found for other characteristics including age and number of days since their last arrest. Furthermore, the study found the homology assumption was violated in 67% of comparisons they made between background characteristics and robbery type. There were some limitations to this study—in particular, the authors stress that only some of the variables highlighted by Alison et al. (2000) were available for the offenders in this sample and that more information could have led to more support for homology. However, the evidence as it stands has failed to find empirical support for homology in robbery offences.

## Reflecting on What This Means

In conclusion, it would appear that there is little empirical support for predictive profiling in robbery. However, whilst the evidence base is sparse, this chapter can hopefully open up a discussion about whether it would be fruitful to conduct research in this area. For example, whilst there is evidence the group dynamics in robbery can complicate the potential to accurately profile offenders, especially if it is unknown which behaviours each offender is displaying (e.g. this could lead to a mixed profile which contains elements from different individuals within the group which could be confusing for an investigation team), the evidence also indicates robbery offences fall into categories (e.g. opportunistic, planned) which can give some indication of background characteristics (e.g. age, criminal experience). Furthermore, if group members behave in a homogenous way (as the evidence would suggest), then this could indicate they share background characteristics. Thus, there may still be potential for predictive profiling to be useful to investigators of personal robbery offences.

## Geographical Profiling

Geographical profiling aims to predict the anchor point (e.g. residence, place of work (Rossmo, 2014)) of offenders using their spatial (and temporal) behaviour (i.e. where and when they commit their offences) (Canter & Gregory, 1994). Rossmo (2000) argues there are a range of investigative uses for geographical profiling. These include suspect prioritisation, task force management, planning patrol strategies, and identifying potential locations of missing persons/bodies.

### *Background*

The relationship between crime and geography is well established—for example, as early as 1942, Shaw and Kay identified that how streets networks are laid out influences spatial patterns in offending—a trend that is reinforced by contemporary work (e.g. Haberman & Kelsay, 2020).

### *Theoretical Framework*

Rooted in environmental criminology (see Brantingham & Brantingham, 1981, 1984), geographical profiling draws on a range of relevant theory. Firstly, there are theories which help to explain how offenders make decisions about where to commit crime. For example, Routine Activity Theory (RAT) (Cohen & Felson, 1979) posits that crime occurs when a motivated offender and suitable target converge in time and space in the absence of a suitable guardian. That is a crime happens when all these elements co-occur (see Fig. 6.1). If this is disrupted, the chances of the crime occurring will reduce (Haberman & Kelsay, 2020) (more on this in Chapter 7).

Rational Choice Theory (RCT) (Cornish & Clarke, 1987) argues that offenders make rational decisions about how, where, and when to commit crime. Geography can feed into this (e.g. target is in a familiar place, there are good escape routes) increasing the opportunities to commit crime. Crime Pattern Theory (CPT) (Brantingham & Brantingham, 1981, 2008) proposes that offenders develop a "mental map" based on their knowledge and understanding of the geographical space (e.g. land use, road networks). Over time, this template becomes fixed (Eck & Weisburd, 2015) and can be used to support later decision making. For example, when the offender comes across a new opportunity to commit crime, they compare the circumstances to their template to determine if it is worth proceeding. Zipf's (1950) Least Effort Principle (i.e. taking the path of least resistance) is also relevant as this helps to explain why people commit crime in places they are familiar with—for example, why commit crime in a new and unusual place when you can commit crime somewhere you are familiar with and know all the escape routes?

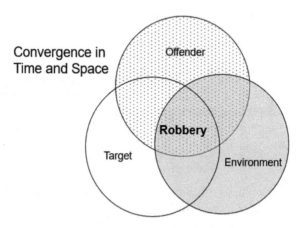

**Fig. 6.1** Routine Activity Theory

For the specific task of predicting the home base (or other anchor point) for offenders, there are two further theories to consider. These are the core assumptions for the technique. Basically, if these don't hold true, geographical profiling won't work. The assumptions are: (1) domocentricity (otherwise known as the Circle Hypothesis) which proposes offenders are more likely to operate close to home than further away (Canter & Larkin, 1993) and (2) distance decay which predicts the probability of committing crime reduces as offenders move further away from home (Brantingham & Brantingham, 1984). The exception to this is the area immediately surrounding the home—Rossmo (2014) argues offenders will avoid this as there is a risk of being recognised. Geographical profilers address this by building in a "buffer zone" (Rossmo, 1997) (i.e. taking into account that offenders are unlikely to commit crime very close to home) when making predictions about where an offender might reside. There is empirical evidence for "buffer zones" where research has found minimum distances from home for where offenders will commit crime (e.g. Canter & Larkin, 1993 [UK sex offences]; Edwards, 2004 [arson in New Zealand]; Górski, 2018 [burglary and robbery in Poland]). However, the buffer zone has not always been found by researchers and concerns have been raised that including the buffer zone could negatively impact on the reliability of profiling (van der Kemp & van Koppen, 2007).

*Evidence for the Assumptions*
Canter and Larkin (1993) proposed a marauder versus commuter model to test the Circle Hypothesis. Marauders operate from their base, moving to and from it to commit offences and staying in close proximity. In contrast, the commuter travels away from his home base to commit his offences. To test this, the crimes and home location of each offender are mapped and a line drawn between the two furthest offences. This forms the diameter of a circle. Results from Canter and Larkin's (1993) study indicated that 87% of offenders (in this case, male sex offenders) fitted the marauder type, i.e. their offences all fell within their circle. This supports the underlying assumption of domocentricity indicating that geographical profiling techniques could be used for this crime type. Evidence of domocentricity has also been found for other offence types such as serial murder (Lundrigan & Canter, 2001). However, the evidence base for property offences is less robust with a lower proportion of offenders fitting into the marauder model. For example, Tonkin et al. (2010) found only 13% of car thieves are marauders. The same has been found in commercial

robbery in Finland where research reported most offenders fitted the commuter model and just 39% of the data conforming to the Circle Hypothesis (Laukkanen & Santtila, 2006). Research in Poland also found a low proportion of robbery offenders were marauders (21%) (Górski, 2018). Furthermore, even the early work on geography (e.g. White, 1932) indicated that property crime offenders are more likely to move out of their neighbourhood to commit crime than those committing crime against people (Edwards, 2004). This is important as it is more difficult to conduct geographical profiling successfully when crime is committed by commuters (Paulson, 2007). Having said this, Laukkanen (2007) argues that knowing whether someone is a marauder or commuter is still helpful as it is possible different search strategies could be implemented to improve the accuracy of profiling based on this.

There is some critique of the Circle Hypothesis as it assumes an equal distribution of offences in all directions. However, it is likely that suitable targets are not distributed evenly (Kocsis et al., 2002) and that offenders' awareness space (i.e. their "mental maps") are not the same (Capone & Nichols, 1975). The type of area should also be considered. For example, Canter and Larkin (1993) themselves noted their hypotheses made no allowances for the local topography of an area or transport routes which could influence how offenders make decisions. Therefore, a circle is not necessarily the most appropriate shape for characterising geographical behaviour. Canter and Larkin (1993) also found the offenders' base was not in the centre of the circle of crimes and propose this could be due to offender learning, with individuals moving further from home as they gain experience, and so indicates that different behavioural models (e.g. marauders, learning) could be interacting. This could impact on geographical profiling as the analyst may need to take this into account when making predictions.

The evidence base for distance decay is more robust. Support for distance decay has been found in studies on a wide range of crime types including burglary (Sarangi & Youngs, 2006) and rape (Santtila et al., 2007). There is some evidence robbers have an environmental range. Early work by Capone and Nichols (1975) examined 825 robbery (commercial and personal) trips in Miami, USA. They found the number of robbery trips decreased sharply as the offender moved further away from home. A third (33%) of trips were within 1 mile of the offender's residence, over half were within 2 miles, and almost two-thirds were within 3 miles. This indicates robbers do not travel far from home to commit their offences. Capone and Nichols (1975) broke their sample down into subsamples including open spaces versus fixed premises locations. If we consider robberies in open spaces to be more indicative of personal robbery (as the offences at fixed premises noted locations such as shops, restaurants, and petrol stations), it is noted that they found shorter robbery trips in these instances. This was explained by an abundance of opportunities meaning this kind of offender does not need to travel far to find a suitable target. Later work by van Koppen and Jansen (1998; commercial robbery in the Netherlands) also found evidence for distance decay although the mean distance travelled was higher (19 km).

It is important to be aware that the journey-to-crime varies by crime type. This means the range of the distance decay might vary depending on the offence. This creates practical challenges for analysts who need to put parameters on their searches (e.g. should they look for the offender's residence within 1 mile of the offence? 5 miles? 10 miles? etc.). Early work by White (1932) found differences across offence types with violent crime occurring closer (0.85 km) than theft offences (e.g. offenders travelled 3.43 km on average to commit car theft). Robbery was 2.14 km on average in this work. Later work also reveals the characteristics of robbery—i.e. armed or not—can influence journey-to-crime with armed offenders travelling further (Capone & Nichols, 1975). Further research has also indicated violent offences (such as rape and murder) tend to be committed closer to home than property offences (such as burglary and armed robbery) (Goodwill et al., 2013). It has also been demonstrated that offences which require more planning have longer journeys-to-crime (Capone & Nichols, 1975; van Koppen & Jansen, 1998).

Offender characteristics—such as age (older offenders travel further; Baldwin & Bottoms, 1976) and experience (as criminal experience increases so does journey-to-crime; van Koppen & Jansen, 1998)—also impact on the journey-to-crime which, in turn, can impact the nature of distance decay (e.g. offending drops off after a longer distance from home than might be expected). This is important as analysts need to set parameters for their searches, and if these are too restrictive, then the possibility of finding the offender's home might be detrimentally affected. The offending situation might also influence journey-to-crime—for example, offenders will travel further if the expected benefits are high (Capone & Nichols, 1975). Group dynamics might also influence journey-to-crime and researchers (e.g. Laukkannen, 2007) have highlighted that spatial behaviour might be influenced by the group (e.g. crime locations may be selected by the group rather than a single offender). Thus, the observed spatial behaviour might not be reflective of an individuals' awareness space and so finding an individual offenders' home location based on crime locations chosen by a group might not be possible. This is, of course, crucial to consider in personal robbery which is largely committed by groups (Burrell et al., 2012; Smith, 2003). It may be that the influence is low if offenders share awareness space and/or live in the same neighbourhood, but this needs to be researched in more depth to understand how distance decay operates for group offences.

There are also concerns about the methods used to test distance decay, specifically whether the actions of an individual offender can be predicted based on distance decay patterns which emerge from research using aggregate data (Smith et al., 2009; van Koppen & De Keijser, 1997). This was tested by van Koppen and De Keijser (1997) who created 1000 hypothetical robbers. Assuming targets were randomly distributed, they randomly simulated crime trips for each offender, ensuring that no individual offender demonstrated distance decay. Despite this, they still found evidence of distance decay when they aggregated the data. They conclude by saying that the assumption distance decay influences individuals is flawed though they do not go so far as to argue that distance decay does not exist based on this evidence. Smith et al. (2009) explored distance decay with UK burglary data finding that, although they observed distance decay at the aggregate level, this did not always translate to the individual level. In sum, it is argued it should not be assumed that distance decay at an individual level exists based on aggregate data. This, of course, has implications for the effectiveness of practice as investigators will be looking to identify home locations for individual perpetrators using geographical profiling techniques.

This is not the only area where aggregation can cause problems. van Wilsem (2009) notes that, as street robbery is geographically concentrated (3% of streets accounted for 48% of street robberies in his sample from the Netherlands), this suggests that opportunities to commit crime are clustered. This means it is unlikely that research can draw any meaningful conclusions about crime variations on an individual level as aggregation means patterns in crime are lost. Robbery is also geographically concentrated in the UK (Chow & Mawby, 2020; Flatley, 2017) indicating this is something to consider in the UK context as well. Further issues are raised by Brantingham et al. (2009) who outline how data is often aggregated for analysis and explain the potential impacts of this when researching spatial relationships. For example, if discrete offences (e.g. robbery or burglary) are collapsed into larger categories (e.g. property crime), then the specific spatial patterns present in that offence type will be lost. In sum, it is difficult to translate evidence from research with aggregate data into practical, real-world investigative techniques that can be used to help identify individual perpetrators.

## Conclusion

Profiling offers some promising and practical techniques that can support investigations. Existing research has established an evidence base for the theoretical frameworks underpinning these techniques. However, it is clear the utility is influenced by crime type (e.g. geographical profiling is more effective for offences predominated by marauders). Furthermore, the use of these techniques with personal robbery is under-researched. Where research has been identified, this has often been related to commercial robbery and/or is not UK based. It is not uncommon for personal and commercial robbery to be combined into a single sample for analysis either making it difficult to unpick the specific results that are the most salient for personal offences. More work in this area would help to understand how profiling techniques might be accurately applied to help identify personal robbery offenders.

## References

Ainsworth, P. B. (2000). *Offender profiling and crime analysis*. Willan Publishing.
Alison, L., Goodwill, A., Almond, L., van den Heuvel, C., & Winter, J. (2011). Pragmatic solutions to offender profiling and behavioural investigative advice. In L. Alison & L. Rainbow (Eds.), *Professionalizing offender profiling: Forensic and investigative psychology in practice* (pp. 51–71). Routledge.
Alison, L., & Rainbow, L. (Eds.). (2011). *Professionalizing offender profiling: Forensic and investigative psychology in practice*. Routledge.
Alison, L., Rockett, W., Deprez, S., & Watts, S. (2000). Bandits, cowboys and Robin's men: The facets of armed robbery. In D. Canter & L. Alison (Eds.), *Profiling property crimes* (pp. 75–106). Ashgate Publishing.
Baldwin, J., & Bottoms, A. E. (1976). *The urban criminal: A study in Sheffield*. Tavistock.
Brantingham, P. J., & Brantingham, P. L. (1981). *Environmental criminology*. Sage.
Brantingham, P. J., & Brantingham, P. L. (1984). *Patterns in crime*. Macmillan.

Brantingham, P., & Brantingham, P. (2008). Crime pattern theory. In R. Wortley & L. Mazerolle (Eds.), *Environmental criminology and crime analysis* (pp. 78–93). Willan Publishing.

Brantingham, P. L., Brantingham, P. J., Vajihollahi, M., & Wuschke, K. (2009). Crime analysis at multiple scales of aggregation: A topological approach. In D. L. Weisburd, W. Bernasco, & G. J. N. Bruinsma (Eds.), *Putting crime in its place: Units of analysis in geographic criminology* (pp. 87–107). Springer.

Burrell, A., Bull, R., & Bond, J. (2012). Linking personal robbery offences using offender behaviour. *Journal of Investigative Psychology and Offender Profiling, 9*(3), 201–222. https://doi.org/10.1002/jip.1365

Canter, D., & Gregory, A. (1994). Identifying the residential location of rapists. *Journal of the Forensic Science Society, 34*, 169–175. https://doi.org/10.1016/S0015-7368(94)72910-8

Canter, D., & Larkin, P. (1993). The environmental range of serial rapists. *Journal of Environmental Psychology, 13*, 63–69. https://doi.org/10.1016/S0272-4944(05)80215-4

Capone, D. L., & Nichols, W. W. (1975). Urban structure and criminal mobility. *American Behavioral Scientist, 20*(2), 199–213.

Chow, L., & Mawby, R. I. (2020). CCTV and robbery in high-rise public housing in Hong Kong. *Safer Communities, 19*(3), 119–130. https://doi.org/10.1108/SC-03-2020-0012

Cohen, L. E., & Felson, M. (1979). Social change and crime rate trends: A routine activity approach. *American Sociological Review, 44*, 588–608. https://doi.org/10.2307/2094589

Cornish, D. B., & Clarke, R. V. (1987). Understanding crime displacement: An application of rational choice theory. *Criminology, 25*, 933–948. https://doi.org/10.1111/j.1745-9125.1987.tb00826.x

Doan, B., & Snook, B. (2008). A failure to find empirical support for the homology assumption in criminal profiling. *Journal of Police and Criminal Psychology, 23*, 61–70. https://doi.org/10.1007/s11896-008-9026-7

Eck, J. E., & Weisburd, D. L. (2015). Crime places in crime theory. *Crime and Place: Crime Prevention Studies, 4*, 1–33.

Edwards, M. J. (2004). *Psychological profiling: Analysing spatial patterns of convicted serial arsonists.* [Masters thesis, University of Canterbury]. https://core.ac.uk/download/pdf/35468068.pdf

Flatley, J. (2017). *Overview of robbery and theft from the person: England and Wales.* Office for National Statistics. https://www.ons.gov.uk/peoplepopulationandcommunity/crimeandjustice/articles/overviewofrobberyandtheftfromtheperson/2017-07-20

Fox, B., & Farrington, D. P. (2018). What have we learned from offender profiling? A systematic review and meta-analysis of 40 years of research.

*Psychological Bulletin, 144*(12), 1247–1274. https://doi.org/10.1037/bul
 0000170
Goodwill, A. M., Stephens, S., Oziel, S., Yapp, J., & Bowes, N. (2012). A multidimensional latent classification of 'street robbery' offences. *Journal of Investigative Psychology and Offender Profiling, 9,* 93–109. https://doi.org/10.1002/jip.1351
Goodwill, A. M., van der Kemp, J. J., & Winter, J. (2013). Applied geographical profiling. In G. J. N. Bruinsma & D. L. Weisburd (Eds.), *Encyclopedia of criminology and criminal justice* (pp. 86–99). Springer.
Górski, M. (2018). Buffer zone and circle theory on the example of burglaries and robberies. *Problems of Forensic Science, 113,* 51–66.
Haberman, C. P., & Kelsay, J. D. (2020). The topography of robbery: Does slope matter? *Journal of Quantitative Criminology.* https://doi.org/10.1007/s10 940-020-09451-z
Harding, S. (2014). *The street casino.* Policy Press.
Harding, S., Deuchar, R., Densley, J., & McLean, R. (2019). A typology of street robbery and gang organization: Insights from qualitative research in Scotland. *British Journal of Criminology, 59,* 879–897. https://doi.org/10.1093/bjc/azy064
Hazelwood, R. R., & Douglas, J. E. (1980). The lust murderer. *FBI Law Enforcement Bulletin, 49,* 18–22.
Herndon, J. S. (2007). The image of profiling: Media treatment and general impressions. In R. N. Kocsis (Ed.), *Criminal profiling: International theory, research, and practice* (pp. 303–323). Humana Press.
Kocsis, R. N., Cooksey, R. W., Irwin, H., & Allen, G. (2002). Further assessment of "circle theory" for geographical psychological profiling. *Australian and New Zealand Journal of Criminology, 35*(1), 43–62. https://doi.org/10.1375/0004865022012
Kocsis, R. N., Irwin, H. J., & Hayes, A. F. (1998). Organised and disorganised criminal behaviour syndromes in arsonists: A validation study of a psychological profiling concept. *Psychiatry, Psychology and Law, 5*(1), 117–131. https://doi.org/10.1080/13218719809524925
Knight, A., & Watson, K. D. (2017). Was Jack the Ripper a slaughterman? Human-animal violence and the world's most infamous serial killer. *Animals, 7*(4), 30. https://doi.org/10.3390/ani7040030
Laukkanen, M. (2007). *Geographic profiling: Using home to crime distances and crime features to predict offender home location.* [Masters thesis, Åbo Akademi University].
Laukkanen, M., & Santtila, P. (2006). Predicting the residential location of a serial commercial robber. *Forensic Science International, 157,* 71–82.

Lundrigan, S., & Canter, D. (2001). A multivariate analysis of serial murderers' disposal site location choice. *Journal of Environmental Psychology, 21*(4), 423–432. https://doi.org/10.1006/jevp.2001.0231

Mokros, A., & Alison, L. (2002). Is offender profiling possible? Testing the predicted homology of crime scene actions and background characteristics in a sample of rapists. *Legal and Criminological Psychology, 7*(1), 25–43. https://doi.org/10.1348/135532502168360

Paulson, D. (2007). Improving geographic profiling through commuter/marauder prediction. *Police Practice & Research, 8*(4), 347–357. https://doi.org/10.1080/15614260701615045

Piotrowski, P. (2011). Street robbery offenders: Shades of rationality and reversal theory. *Rationality and Society, 23*(4), 427–451. https://doi.org/10.1177/1043631114114125

Porter, L. E., & Alison, L. J. (2006a). Behavioural coherence in group robbery: A circumplex model of offender and victim interactions. *Aggressive Behavior, 32*, 330–342. https://doi.org/10.1002/ab.20132

Porter, L. E., & Alison, L. J. (2006b). Leadership and hierarchies in criminal groups: Scaling degrees of leader behaviour in group robbery. *Legal & Criminological Psychology, 11*, 234–265. https://doi.org/10.1348/135532 50568692

Rainbow, L. (2011). Taming the beast: The UK approach to the management of behavioural investigative advice. In L. Alison & L. Rainbow (Eds.), *Professionalizing offender profiling: Forensic and investigative psychology in practice* (pp. 5–17). Routledge.

Rainbow, L., Almond, L., & Alison, L. (2011). BIA support to investigative decision making. In L. Alison & L. Rainbow (Eds.), *Professionalizing offender profiling: Forensic and investigative psychology in practice* (pp. 35–50). Routledge.

Rainbow, L., & Gregory, A. (2011). What behavioural investigative advisors actually do. In L. Alison & L. Rainbow (Eds.), *Professionalizing offender profiling: Forensic and investigative psychology in practice* (pp. 18–34). Routledge.

Rossmo, D. K. (1997). Geographic profiling. In J. L. Jackson & D. A. Bekerian (Eds.), *Offender profiling: Theory, research and practice* (pp. 159–175). John Wiley & Sons.

Rossmo, K. (2000). *Geographical profiling*. CRC Press.

Rossmo, D. K. (2014). Geographic profiling. In G. Bruinsma & D. Weisburd (Eds.), *Encyclopedia of criminology and criminal justice* (pp. 1934–1942). Springer.

Santtila, P., Laukkkanen, M., & Zappalà, A. (2007). Crime behaviours and distance travelled in homicides and rapes. *Journal of Investigative Psychology and Offender Profiling, 4*(1), 1–15. https://doi.org/10.1002/jip.56

Sarangi, S., & Youngs, D. (2006). Spatial patterns of Indian serial burglars with relevance to geographical profiling. *Journal of Investigative Psychology and Offender Profiling, 3*(2), 105–115. https://doi.org/10.1002/jip.38

Shaw, C. R., & McKay, H. D. (1942). *Juvenile delinquency and urban areas*. University of Chicago Press.

Smith, M. J. (2003). The nature of personal robbery. *Home Office Research Study 254*. Home Office.

Smith, W. R., Bond, J. W., & Townsley, M. (2009). Determining how journeys-to-crime vary: Measuring inter- and intra-offender crime trip distributions. In D. L. Weisburd, W. Bernasco, & G. J. N. Bruinsma (Eds.), *Putting crime in its place: Units of analysis in geographic criminology* (pp. 217–236). Springer.

Tonkin, M., Woodhams, J., Bond, J. W., & Loe, T. (2010). A theoretical and practical test of geographical profiling with serial vehicle theft in a UK context. *Behavioral Sciences and the Law, 28*(3), 442–460. https://doi.org/10.1002/bsl.916

van der Kemp, J. J., & van Koppen, P. J. (2007). Fine-tuning geographical profiling. In R. N. Kocsis (Ed.), *Criminal profiling: International theory, research, and practice* (pp. 347–366). Humana Press.

van Koppen, P., & Jansen, R. (1998). The road to robbery: Travel patterns in commercial robberies. *British Journal of Criminology, 38*(2), 230–246.

van Koppen, P. J., & De Keijser, J. (1997). Desisting distance decay: In the aggregation of individual crime trips. *Criminology, 35*(3), 505–515.

van Wilsem, J. (2009). Urban streets as micro contexts to commit violence. In D. L. Weisburd, W. Bernasco, & G. J. N. Bruinsma (Eds.), *Putting crime in its place: Units of analysis in geographic criminology* (pp. 199–216). Springer.

Walsh, D. (1986). *Heavy business: Commercial burglary and robbery*. Routledge.

White, R. C. (1932). The relation of felonies to environmental factors in Indianapolis. *Social Forces, 10*, 459–467.

Woodhams, J., & Toye, K. (2007). An empirical test of the assumptions of case linkage and offender profiling with serial commercial robberies. *Psychology, Public Policy and Law, 13*, 59–85. https://doi.org/10.1037/1076-8971.13.1.59

Yapp, J. R. (2010). *The profiling of robbery offenders*. [ForenPsyD thesis, University of Birmingham]. https://etheses.bham.ac.uk/id/eprint/1059/1/Yapp10ForenPsyD.pdf

Zipf, G. (1950). *The principle of least effort*. Addison Wesley.

CHAPTER 7

# Policing and Prevention

**Abstract** This chapter will summarise policing tactics used to prevent and/or reduce robbery. This includes discussion of education and diversion, situational approaches (which are designed to reduce the opportunities to commit crime), and police approaches and tactics. Offender-based interventions are also discussed. Furthermore, large-scale police and partnership work—such as the Street Crime Initiative and the Public Health Approach—will be outlined.

**Keywords** Robbery · Policing · Prevention · Situational crime prevention · Public health approach

## INTRODUCTION

This chapter will outline some of the approaches used to try to prevent and/or reduce personal robbery. Tackling robbery can have a diffusion of benefits effect. For example, Stripe (2021) found that a reduction in knife-enabled robbery led to an overall reduction in knife crime in England and Wales (year ending December 2020) indicating how relevant tackling robbery is to reducing other offending (in this case, knife crime). Furthermore, many robbers are repeat offenders with a third of robbers re-offending within 12 months of release from prison (Ministry of Justice,

© The Author(s), under exclusive license to Springer Nature Switzerland AG 2022
A. Burrell, *Robbery*,
https://doi.org/10.1007/978-3-030-93173-5_7

2020). There are also high levels of reconviction (Travers et al., 2015). Therefore, targeting prolific offenders is often seen as central to crime reduction activity (Tilley et al., 2004). Thus, tackling robbery by apprehending, convicting, and/or managing offenders effectively can result in reductions in offending. If this work includes treatment—for example, focusing on breaking the cycle of offending—this can have long-term positive impacts for the offender and society as a whole.

The different approaches used to tackle robbery are presented chronologically across the offenders' journey starting with education and diversion. Situational Crime Prevention—which is designed to reduce the opportunities to commit crime—is outlined followed by police approaches and tactics. Next, offender-based interventions are discussed. Finally, the Public Health Approach to reducing violence is introduced with some discussion around how this might be helpful to target robbery.

## Early Intervention

Policing is founded on the principle of prevention. This was Robert Peel's key principle when setting up the Metropolitan Police in 1829 (Lentz & Chaires, 2007). For robbery (as with other violent offences), prevention work centres around early intervention (e.g. through education and diversion). Programmes are not necessarily focused on robbery, but they do often aim to work with those individuals at risk of committing robbery offences.

### *Education and Diversion Programmes*

Educational programmes are seen as essential for preventing crime and promoting a culture of lawfulness (UNDOC, 2017). There are a number of examples of targeted educational programmes being introduced in schools in the UK and school-based programmes remain popular—see, for example, the toolkit outlining interventions to prevent school exclusion (which are designed to indirectly prevent youth offending) (Gaffney et al., 2021). These are designed to reach young people before they become involved in offending behaviour and can be introduced as early as primary school (Home Office, n.d.; Waddell, 2020) but should be built into all levels of education (i.e. primary, secondary, tertiary; UNDOC, 2017).

Another option is diversionary activities—for example, via youth crime prevention programmes. These are often targeted at young people who have been in trouble with the police, are assessed as being "at risk" of committing crime, and/or are involved in anti-social behaviour (Gov.uk, 2021). The aim is to engage young people in activities which keep them away from crime, but they might also learn new skills which will then help them to engage with education or find a job (Gov.uk, 2021). Mentoring approaches are popular and have been demonstrated to have some success (College of Policing, 2016). With regard to group effects, research has found contact between groups can reduce intergroup prejudice (Pettigrew & Tropp, 2011) and so it is not surprising that there are also programmes which work to break down barriers between young people and help them to find common ground which would be useful to help tackle ingroup versus outgroup conflict.

Education and diversionary work is unlikely to be focused specifically on robbery but can be aimed to prevent violence and so may have a positive effect on robbery rates. Thus, they are useful to consider as part of a multi-faceted crime prevention/reduction initiative, especially if they target topics around group dynamics/peer pressure.

## SITUATION-BASED APPROACHES

Environmental approaches to crime prevention focus on how the environment or situation influences the offender's decision to commit crime (Swanson & Livingstone, 2020). Key theories include Rational Choice Theory (RCT) (Cornish & Clarke, 1986) and Routine Activity Theory (RAT) (Cohen & Felson, 1979). RCT is grounded in rationality arguing the offender makes active, informed choices, and that offenders will commit crime when the rewards outweigh the risks (see Fig. 7.1).

In short, if the offender believes they can successfully commit an offence without being caught, then the chances are they will take the opportunity (Kitteringham & Fennelly, 2020). Critics of RCT argue that it does not account for context—for example, the situation the offender finds themselves in. RCT has been also critiqued for overestimating the extent to which offenders weigh up the risks and rewards of committing crime (Renzetti, 2008). For example, how "rational" is a dependent drug user who is experiencing withdrawal when making decisions? However, it is argued that the underlying assumption of RCT is choices and decisions happen, no matter how rudimentary or flawed (Cornish & Clarke, 1986).

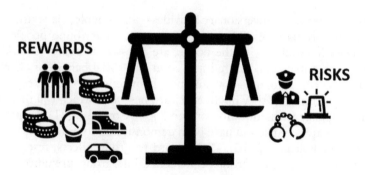

**Fig. 7.1** Rational Choice Theory—risks outweigh rewards

RAT posits that offenders see opportunities to commit crime in their everyday life (i.e. as they are going about their regular routine activities). RAT has been also critiqued for its assumption that offenders are rational decision makers (Kitteringham & Fennelly, 2020). This is perhaps not surprising when you consider RAT was developed using RCT principles. However, the benefit of these theories is that they have been used to develop practical tools to help reduce crime. In particular, RAT has been used to develop the Problem Analysis Crime Triangle (Clarke & Eck, 2003). This posits that a crime will take place when three elements come together in time and space—(1) a motivated offender, (2) a suitable target, and (3) the absence of a capable guardian (see Fig. 7.2).

With reference to robbery, Monk et al. (2010: 10) state that "Street robberies occur when motivated offenders encounter suitable victims in an environment that facilitates robbery". This is the application of the Problem Analysis Crime Triangle to robbery and helps the investigator start to think about how they might disrupt offending. See, for example, Fig. 7.3.

Add to this RCT and the investigator is encouraged to "think thief" (i.e. consider opportunities from the offenders' perspective) (Clarke & Eck, 2003; Felson & Clarke, 1998), and a range of situation-based opportunities to prevent and disrupt offending can be developed. This Situational Crime Prevention (SCP) approach encompasses a range of practical options under five key themes—(1) increase the effort it takes to commit crime, (2) increase the risks of committing crime, (3) reduce the rewards, (4) reduce provocations that can facilitate offending, and (5) remove excuses for offending (Cornish & Clarke, 2003). Some examples of how

**Fig. 7.2** Problem Analysis Crime Triangle

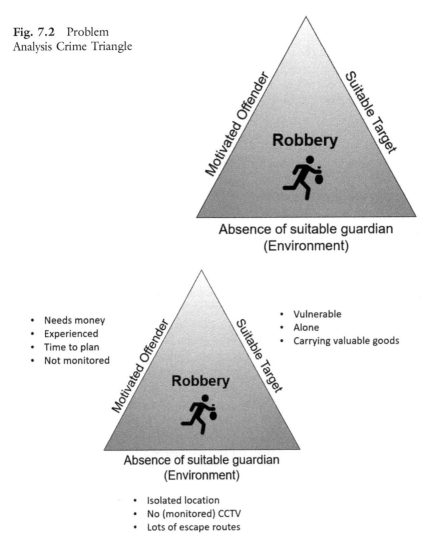

**Fig. 7.3** Using the Crime Triangle to understand robbery

this might apply to robbery include automatic phone disablers (making it difficult for offenders to sell on goods, i.e. increasing the effort), the use of CCTV and/or lighting (increase the risk), disrupting stolen goods markets (reduce rewards), neutralising peer pressure (remove provocation), and controlling substances (remove excuses). A few of these examples are now discussed in more detail.

### *Increase the Risk: CCTV*

Closed Circuit Television (CCTV) is a traditional crime prevention measure. A recent meta-analysis (of 76 studies) concluded that CCTV is associated with decreases in crime (Piza et al., 2019). However, evidence on its impact on reducing crime is not clear-cut. For example, reductions in crime are not always observed (Gill & Spriggs, 2005), appear more effective in certain types of places (e.g. car parks) (Farrington et al., 2007; Gill & Spriggs, 2005), and do not impact on all crime types (Farrington et al., 2007) including violent crime (College of Policing, 2013).

There are several ways CCTV can be utilised to tackle robbery. Firstly, it can be used to help identify perpetrators post-offence (Monk et al., 2010). Secondly, in some instances, it can help reduce crime. For example, the deployment of mobile CCTV has been associated with a 20% reduction in street robbery (Burrows et al., 2003). Targeted CCTV use in response to very specific crime problems has also been demonstrated to be valuable—for example, in recent research from Hong Kong, CCTV was successfully used to reduce robbery offences in the elevators of tower blocks (with no evidence that these offences were displaced elsewhere) (Chow & Mawby, 2020). Piza et al. (2019) identified that CCTV schemes which involved active (rather than passive) monitoring and those combined with other crime prevention measures are the most effective. Furthermore, CCTV is most useful for planned (rather than spontaneous) offending (Piza et al., 2019).

### *Reduce Rewards: Disruption of Stolen Goods Markets*

Items which are CRAVED—i.e. concealable, removable, available, valuable, enjoyable, and disposable—are attractive to thieves (Clarke & Eck, 2003; Wellsmith & Burrell, 2005). Crime prevention efforts can focus on manipulating these characteristics—for example, if items are concealed (e.g. in a pocket or bag), it is harder for the offender to reach these during the robbery (thus, increasing the effort needed to commit the offence). Another method is to manipulate the disposability of the item (Wellsmith & Burrell, 2005). The Market Reduction Approach (Sutton, 1998) makes handling stolen goods more risky (e.g. more regulation of pawn shops) and so buyers might not be willing to pay as much for the item. This, therefore, reduces the rewards for the offender. For robbery, if there are particular items being stolen, it is argued targeting where these might be sold on could help increse the risks and reduce the rewards for offenders. For example, high value pedal cycles—the robbery of expensive bicycles (sometimes by heavily armed offenders on mopeds) has been reported in the news (see, for example, Ormiston, 2021).

## Policing Strategies/Tactics

The police have implemented a range of strategies to tackle robbery including robbery teams, patrolling, and stop and search. Police have also been key partners in multi-agency initiatives—the best known being the Street Crime Initiative (SCI). All of these approaches will be outlined and discussed.

### *Robbery Teams*

Many police forces have employed "Robbery Teams" or taskforces over the years to specifically tackle robbery. Perhaps the best known in the UK is the Flying Squad, a specialist unit of the Metropolitan Police with a remit to tackle armed robbery (Matthews, 2002). The focus was on planned, organised, and professional robberies and so the squad focus on commercial robbery. However, dedicated teams have also been set up in local areas with robbery as a specific part of their remit—for example, the High Harm and Robbery Team at West Midlands Police. Monk et al. (2010) advocate dedicated teams, for example, explaining that targeted patrols can operate better when part of a "robbery task force".

### *Patrolling*

Research can be used to inform police decision making in relation to patrol strategies—for example, identifying where and when offences are most likely to occur (Wüllenweber & Burrell, 2020). Research from the USA (using agent-based modelling to simulate the impact of patrolling on robbery) has indicated that being more focused in where police officers patrol (e.g. targeting known hotspots) can help reduce crime (Wooditch, 2021). Furthermore, the research found that if one-third of officers' time was spend on proactive work, this could result in substantial reductions in robbery (Wooditch, 2021). High visibility patrols have been shown to successfully deter robbery offenders (Jones & Tilley, 2004). In this instance, additional foot patrols were added on Friday and Saturday nights in Hull (UK) and data indicated robbery fell by 16% compared to the previous year and against a national upward trend (Jones & Tilley, 2004). Monk et al. (2010) report directed patrols appear to deter street robbers, work best as part of a dedicated task force, and should be guided by detailed crime analysis of robbery hotspots and hot times. They also advocate combining patrols with other measures (such as awareness campaigns) to maximise impact (ibid.). However, other research (from the USA) has indicated that street robbery is displaced (both spatially and temporally) by saturation foot patrols and suggests that this needs to be considered when designing such initiatives (Piza & O'Hara, 2014). Covert patrolling can also be useful, in particular to help catch offenders. The Metropolitan Police (London, UK) implemented covert patrols alongside high visibility patrols. Research found a 30% increase in people charged with robbery after 1 year (Monk et al., 2010).

### *Stop and Search*

Police have the power to stop and search individuals under the Police and Criminal Evidence Act (PACE) 1984. This provides the police with powers to stop and search citizens if they have "reasonable grounds" to suspect they are carrying illegal drugs, weapon(s), stolen property, or something which could be used to commit crime (e.g. a crowbar for burglary) (UK Government, 2021a). Section 60 enhances these powers to allow authorisation for stop and search without reasonable grounds (Home Office, 2014). This has to be approved by a senior officer and can happen if it is suspected that (1) serious violence could occur, (2) someone is carrying a weapon or has used one, or (3) someone is in a specific location or area (e.g. where a crime has just taken place) (UK Government, 2021a). For example, authorisation could be given if there was a significant increase in robberies in a particular area (Home Office, 2014) and so this is a tactic which has been implemented to try to address street robbery.

There were 563,837 stop and searches in England and Wales between April 2019 and March 2020 (UK Government, 2021b). The highest rate of stop and search is in London where there are 34 per 1,000 people, and almost half of all stop and searches were carried out by the Metropolitan Police (UK Government, 2021b). There has been criticism of the way stop and search has been implemented, in particular the disproportionate use of stop and search with ethnic minority groups (Bowling & Phillips, 2007; Equality and Human Rights Commission, 2010). The discriminatory use of stop and search has been especially documented as used against Black individuals who are 6 times more likely to be stopped and searched than White people (Equality and Human Rights Commission, 2010). In London, Black people under 18 represent 37% of stop and searches despite only making up 15% of the population (UK Parliament, 2007). Recent statistics indicate this remains an issue with 54 stop and searches recorded per 1,000 Black people in England and Wales compared to just 6 per 1,000 people for White individuals (UK Government, 2021b).

Some arguments have been put forward for why stop and search is disproportionate. In relation to robbery, for example, arrest statistics—which show Black individuals are more likely to be arrested for street robbery (Bowling & Phillips, 2007; UK Parliament, 2007)—are used to justify higher stop and search rates (Bowling & Phillips, 2007; Equality and Human Rights Commission, 2010). However, it is argued that stereotypes are leading to assumptions that all young Black people are involved in crime, in particular robbery (Bowling & Phillips, 2007). Other ethnic minority groups are also overrepresented in stop and search—e.g. Asian people are twice as likely to be stopped and searched as White people (Equality and Human Rights Commission, 2010).

Aside from the criticism surrounding the discriminatory application of stop and search (which can alienate communities and negatively impact on perceptions of the police), there is also the issue of whether it actually works to help reduce robbery. It is argued that robbery (along with other violent offences, drug dealing, and theft) is more susceptible to stop and search tactics as they involve carrying items related to committing the offence (e.g. weapons) (Tiratelli et al., 2018). In the USA, for example, MacDonald et al. (2016) reported a reduction in robbery was associated with the introduction of "stop, question, frisks" (SQFs); however, they could not directly attribute stops to the reductions. Smith et al. (2012 cited in Tiratelli et al., 2018) found no significant reductions in robbery once confounding variables had been accounted for. Research in the UK has also struggled to find direct links between reductions in robbery and stop and search tactics, in this case large-scale increases in searches for weapons (Operation BLUNT2) (McCandless et al., 2016). A recent analysis of 10 years' worth of London-wide data also found no evidence of effects of stop and search on robbery (Tiratelli et al., 2018). More research is needed to determine if (1) stop and search can help prevent and/or reduce crime and (2) if it is, under what circumstances it is most effective (e.g. targeting particular crime types, reason for suspicion, level of evidence for grounds to search, etc.).

### *Street Crime Initiative*

The Street Crime Initiative (SCI) was launched in 2002 in England and Wales in response to increasing levels of robbery (Tilley et al., 2004). SCI focused on "street crime" explaining this encompassed both robbery and snatch theft and focused on the 10 police forces which together accounted for 83% of robbery (in 2001/2002). The SCI was a multi-agency run programme of work which recognised there is no single method for reducing crime. Instead, it offered a suite of options and guidance on how to develop further crime prevention initiatives using a problem-solving approach (Tilley et al., 2004). There were significant reductions in robbery in the police forces where the SCI ran in comparison with forces where the SCI was not implemented (Home Office, 2003; Machin & Marie, 2011). Furthermore, SCI was demonstrated to be a cost-effective intervention (Machin & Marie, 2011). Improvements made as a result of the SCI (and cited as central to success) included improved partnership working, better data collection and analysis of robbery, and more effective implementation of tactics to apprehend offenders (Home Office, 2003). It is also noted, however, that more funds and better access to services (e.g. diversionary activities for young people and access to drug treatment) were reported during the SCI (Home Office, 2003) which highlights the practical benefits of having a dedicated fund available to tackle street crime.

### *New and Emerging Technologies*

Emerging technologies can increase opportunities to commit crime (there is some discussion of this in **Chapter 2**). However, it can also present new opportunities to prevent crime and/or identify perpetrators. For example, Farrell (2015) outlines the potential for using kill switches (where devices are switched off remotely) to help prevent mobile phone theft and robbery. McCardie et al. (2011) outline a range of design elements that could be built into mobile phones to help reduce their attractiveness to robbers. They also asked offenders (and non-offenders) if they would be deterred by these measures reporting that offenders would be deterred by technological design elements such as biometric activation (82%) and trackers (79%). Technological solutions are being actively sought to help reduce robbery—for example, Wang et al. (2020) are working to design a portable personal security device and testing this in street robbery scenarios.

*Facial Recognition and "Super-Recognisers"*
Facial recognition can be key to identify offenders and software has been developed to help this work. However, research has shown that people can be very poor at matching faces to photos (Robertson et al., 2016), especially if they are matching an unfamiliar face to low-quality CCTV images (Henderson et al., 2001). Facial recognition is still very error prone even when higher-quality images are provided (ibid.). However, facial matching skills have also been demonstrated to be open to wide variation and some people are excellent at this task (Robertson et al., 2016). These people are known as "Super-Recognisers" (Robertson et al., 2016) and have even been shown to perform better than biometric facial recognition systems (Ring, 2016). Dedicated police teams of such people have been set up (Edmund & Wortley, 2016) and can work to proactively identify offenders. For example, police super-recognisers might identify the same individual in multiple images (e.g. of robberies) which can help link offences and provide leads for investigators (Edmund & Wortley, 2016).

Research has found that police super-recognisers perform far better than normal with both familiar and unfamiliar faces even with degraded images (Robertson et al., 2016). For example, Ring (2016) reports that police super-recognisers make hundreds of suspect identifications for each individual identification made by a computer system. Thus, it is suggested that continuing to recruit people with these skills is an efficient way to improve facial recognition work (Robertson et al., 2016).

## Offender-Based Approaches

### Incarceration

The most obvious way to prevent robbery is the capture and imprison offenders. The maximum sentence is life imprisonment, an unlimited fine, or both (Crown Prosecution Service, 2019). The scale of the sentence varies by circumstance and takes culpability and level of harm into account (Sentencing Council, 2021). Offences which have high culpability (e.g. use of a weapon, use of significant force) and/or high harm (e.g. serious physical or psychological injury) will attract higher sentences (see Sentencing Council, 2021 for a breakdown). The average length of a custodial sentence for robbery in 2019/2020 in England and Wales was 51.6 months (Clark, 2021). England and Wales have one of the highest imprisonment rates in Europe (Prison Reform Trust, 2019) with 78,830 men and women in prison as of September 2021 (Ministry of Justice and Her Majesty's Prison and Probation Service, 2021). Around 10% of the adults in custody and around a quarter of juveniles were serving sentences relating to robbery in March 2020 (Sturge, 2020).

There is controversy about the effectiveness of incarceration. Almost half of adults and 65% of children re-offend within 12 months of release (Prison Reform Trust, 2019). For robbery, re-offending statistics for January-March 2018 indicate that around 30% of adults and just over 40% of juveniles were proven to have re-offended in England and Wales (Ministry of Justice, 2020). Furthermore, a reconviction rate of 53% was found in a sample of over 3,000 robbery offenders (Travers et al., 2015). This suggests that, whilst prison can prevent the immediate crimes an offender might commit, this would not last beyond the length of the sentence without other interventions. The next few sections will discuss other offender-based approaches to prevention.

### Offender Management

Integrated Offender Management (IOM) is a multi-agency approach which aims to support prolific offenders to stop committing crime (Home Office and Ministry of Justice, 2015). It provides a holistic package of support to offenders and is used with robbery offenders (HM Government, 2020); in fact, IOM was originally designed for acquisitive offenders (Her Majesty's Inspectorate of Probation, 2021). Hutchinson (2020) argues that joint working has enhanced our understanding of offender motivation which feeds into the development of new crime reduction initiatives. Evaluations of the impact of IOM have produced mixed results (Her Majesty's Inspectorate of Probation, 2021), and a recent inspection has reported that, although there are indications that IOM can have a positive impact, there is no comprehensive evidence for its effectiveness (HM Inspectorate of Probation and HM Inspectorate of Constabulary and Fire & Rescue Service, 2020). The report included a useful case example of how an offender who committed robbery (as well as other offences) was supported by his IOM team but did not extend so far as to report this individuals' recidivism outcomes (ibid.). A recent systematic review into the effectiveness of IOM has found that, although the key principles of IOM have been largely incorporated into local schemes, evidence for a reduction in re-offending is lacking (Hadfield et al., 2021).

## Treatment and Rehabilitation

Another way to approach tackling offending is to work with robbers themselves to help them change their attitudes with the view to curbing their offending. Rehabilitation programmes aim to support the offender to reconnect with society (e.g. building relationships, getting a job, etc.) with the view of moving towards being crime-free (Hollin & Palmer, 2020). The names of individual programmes may change, but the overarching principles are often similar. In particular, many offender behaviour programmes draw on the "Risk, Needs, Responsivity" (RNR) approach (Hollin & Palmer, 2020), which is the most prominent model of treatment in the world (Her Majesty's Inspectorate of Probation, 2020). The Risk-Need model (Andrews & Bonta, 1994) indicates that offenders have two types of needs—criminogenic and non-criminogenic. Criminogenic needs (e.g. anti-social peer groups, substance use) need to be addressed to reduce offending behaviour (Hollin & Palmer, 2020). RNR builds on this to identify who to target (risk), what should be done (need), and how to achieve this (responsivity) (Her Majesty's Inspectorate of Probation, 2020). Reductions in offending have been achieved when implementing RNR principles—for example, it has been associated with a 17% reduction in average recidivism in custody settings and 35% in community environments (Her Majesty's Inspectorate of Probation, 2020).

## Cognitive Skills Programmes

Some programmes are focused on particular offence types, and others concentrate on developing more general competencies such as thinking skills and reasoning (Hollin & Palmer, 2020). There are no well-established programmes specifically targeting property crime offenders (Hollin & Palmer, 2020) although there are some which focus on violent crime (which could include robbery) and others which are available to all offenders. General offender programmes include "Reasoning and Rehabilitation" (R&R), and "Enhanced Thinking Skills" (ETS), both of which aim to change cognitive functioning (Hollin & Palmer, 2009). R&R was designed by Ross and Fabiano (1985) and delivered learning around social-perspective taking, social problem solving, and critical thinking skills in a structured groupwork environment (Hollin & Palmer, 2020). Evaluations of this programme have revealed significant decreases in re-offending for participants compared to control groups and have been shown to be effective in the UK (Tong & Farrington, 2006). One note of caution though is that this meta-analysis revealed no significant improvements for robbers undertaking R&R in Canada (Tong & Farrington, 2006). ETS was developed by the English and Welsh Prison Service (Clark, 2000 cited in Hollin & Palmer, 2020). The aim is the same as R&R and it also uses a cognitive-behavioural approach. However, it is shorter being delivered across 20 two-hour sessions (Hollin & Palmer, 2020) (compared to 36 two-hour sessions for R&R; Tong & Farrington, 2006). An evaluation of this programme indicated reductions in recidivism but not for robbery offenders (Travers et al., 2015). It was concluded that addressing other needs—such as financial motivation, substance misuse, and/or pro-criminal attitudes—might be a more appropriate approach for robbery offenders (Travers et al., 2015). Other explanations for why cognitive skills programmes might not work for robbery offenders include lower levels of motivation to engage and/or that pro-criminal attitudes are more ingrained (Wilson et al., 2003)—an argument which is supported by Motiuk and Porporino's (1991) work which found robbers had higher rates of diagnosis for anti-social behaviour disorder. It is also possible that robbers have higher levels of psychopathy relative to other offenders (Hare et al., 2000) which could impede the effectiveness of programmes (Rice et al., 1992).

*Addressing the Group Dynamic*
Research has highlighted that group offending differs from lone offending (e.g. Alarid et al., 2009; Burrell et al., 2015) and this needs to be considered when developing criminal justice interventions (van Mastrigt & Farrington, 2009), and when risk assessing offenders (da Silva et al., 2013). Etgar and Prager (2009) note that group offenders are in need of special treatment. For example, it is known that group offenders are at a higher risk of co-offending (Hodgson, 2007) and so group offenders need to be treated in group therapies that address group dynamics (Etgar & Prager, 2009). However, Wüllenweber and Burrell (2020) argue that, due to differences between offence behaviours across different group sizes, consideration may need to be given as to how to adapt treatment (e.g. co-dependence between two people might need to be treated differently to work to support individuals in larger offending groups to resist peer pressure or follow a charismatic leader).

*Drug Treatment*
Drug misuse is associated with criminal behaviour (Guimarães et al., 2017) including robbery (Stockdale & Gresham, 1998) with some offenders reporting committing street robbery to support a drug habit (Tilley et al., 2004). It is not surprising, therefore, that drug treatment is often recommended as a potential tactic to help reduce re-offending (Mawby et al., 2007; Rajkumar & French, 1997; Tilley et al., 2004). Furthermore, Tilley and colleagues (2004) argue that enforcement without treatment is unlikely to be successful at reducing recidivism for dependent drug users. There have been some promising results of drug treatment programmes—for example, a study from the USA found that substance abuse treatment was associated with significant reductions in armed robbery (Basu et al., 2008). Similar outcomes have been reported in the UK with interviews with offenders finding self-reports of street robbery reduced by two-thirds following drug treatment (Sondhi et al., 2002). It is noted, however, that this outcome was not found for all groups with some offenders less likely to engage in treatment. For example, it was found that young, male, crack using street robbers was one of the groups least likely to engage with a programme of referral to treatment upon arrest (Sondhi et al., 2002). Non-engagement and drop out is a problem for drug treatment (Tilley et al., 2004) which has led to some initiatives offering more wraparound support (in the form of housing, education) as part of a "carrot and stick" approach (Tilley et al.,

2004). This acts by pulling levers—that is, if they disengage from the programme or restart offending, they are actively pursued for all criminal activities (Tilley et al., 2004).

Where drug treatment is successful, there are economic benefits to this (Basu et al., 2008). There are also social benefits, i.e. through the reduction in offending (Rajkumar & French, 1997). In the UK, the economic and social benefit of arrest referral schemes is reported to be in the region of 7 to 1 with additional benefits if treatment is sustained over time (Sondhi et al., 2002).

### A Public Health Approach

The public health approach to reducing violence is a whole-system multi-agency approach to preventing serious violence (Public Health England, 2019). This approach does not focus on robbery specifically, but this is one of the violent offences that is included under the remit of such work (see, for example, Wolf et al., 2014). A range of initiatives have been rolled out in the UK to support delivery of a public health approach— for example, statutory duties for public sector agencies to prevent serious violence and the setup of Violence Reduction Units (VRUs). There is a growing literature in this area, but there have already been some reports of this approach having a positive impact—for example, the Local Government Association (2020) has published a series of case studies. A former robber also discusses his positive experiences of receiving support from a VRU on the Place2Be website (Silverton, 2020). Furthermore, it is a recommended approach for tackling a range of issues including community violence (Decker et al., 2018), domestic violence (Chandan et al., 2020), and violent extremism (Weine et al., 2017). It is perhaps not surprising that a public health approach is being advocated as research has demonstrated links between health and income inequality and crime (including robbery) (Wolf et al., 2014). Overall, it is argued that the public health approach demonstrates a positive route to support crime reduction, including robbery offending.

## Conclusion

This chapter has summarised a range of approaches for tackling robbery. These range from situational crime prevention to try and reduce opportunities for offending to enforcement action designed to take offenders off the street. There are a variety of measures and these can be used in combination to try to maximise outcomes. It is not surprising, therefore, that a number of the initiatives discussed include multi-faceted, multi-agency approaches. Offending is complex and there are a range of reasons why people commit crime. Concentrating on developing more dynamic, needs-based, interventions—for example, the public health approach—appears to be one promising action going forward to prevent robbery.

## REFERENCES

Alarid, L. F., Burton, V. S., & Hochstetler, A. L. (2009). Group and solo robberies: Do accomplices shape criminal form? *Journal of Criminal Justice, 37*, 1–9. https://doi.org/10.1016/j.jcrimjus.2008.12.001

Andrews, D. A., & Bonta, J. (1994). *The psychology of criminal conduct*. Anderson Publishing.

Basu, A., Paltiel, A. D., & Pollack, H. A. (2008). Social costs of robbery and the cost-effectiveness of substance misuse treatment. *Health Economics, 17*, 927–946. https://doi.org/10.1002/hec.1305

Bowling, B., & Phillips, C. (2007). Disproportionate and discriminatory: Reviewing the evidence on police stop and search. *The Modern Law Review, 70*(6), 936–961. https://doi.org/10.1111/j.1468-2230.2007.00671.x

Burrell, A., Bull, R., Bond, J., & Herrington, G. (2015). Testing the impact of group offending on behavioural similarity in serial robbery. *Psychology, Crime & Law, 21*(6), 551–569. https://doi.org/10.1080/1068316X.2014.999063

Burrows, J., Poole, H., Read, T., & Webb, S. (2003). *Tackling personal robbery: Lessons learnt from the police and community safety partnerships* (No. 5). Home Office.

Chandan, J. S., Taylor, J., Bradbury-Jones, C., Nirantharakumar, N., Kane, E., & Bandyopadhyay, S. (2020). COVID-19: A public health approach to manage domestic violence is needed. *The Lancet Public Health, 5*(6). Published online May 8. https://doi.org/10.1016/S2468-2667(20)30112-2

Chow, L., & Mawby, R. I. (2020). CCTV and robbery in high-rise public housing in Hong Kong. *Safer Communities, 19*(3), 119–130. https://doi.org/10.1108/SC-03-2020-0012

Clark, D. (2021). *Average length of prison sentences for offences in England and Wales 2020*. https://www.statista.com/statistics/1100192/prison-sentence-length-in-england-and-wales-by-offence/

Clarke, R. V., & Eck, J. (2003). *How to become a problem solving crime analyst*. Jill Dando Institute of Crime Science.

Cohen, L. E., & Felson, M. (1979). Social change and crime rate trends: A routine activity approach. *American Sociological Review, 44*, 588–608. https://doi.org/10.2307/2094589

College of Policing. (2013). *The effects of CCTV on crime: What works briefing*. https://www.raggeduniversity.co.uk/wp-content/uploads/2016/12/What-works-briefing-effects-of-CCTV-2013.pdf

College of Policing. (2016). *Mentoring*. https://whatworks.college.police.uk/toolkit/Pages/Intervention.aspx?InterventionID=44

Cornish, D. B., & Clarke, R. (1986). *The reasoning criminal: Rational choice perspectives on offending*. Springer-Verlag.

Cornish, D. B., & Clarke, R. (2003). Opportunities, precipitators and criminal decisions: A reply to Wortley's critique of situational crime prevention. In M. Smith & D. Cornish (Eds.), *Theory and practice in situational crime prevention* (pp. 41–96). Criminal Justice Press.

Crown Prosecution Service. (2019). *Theft Act Offences*. https://www.cps.gov.uk/legal-guidance/theft-act-offences

da Silva, T., Woodhams, J., & Harkins, L. (2013). Heterogeneity within multiple perpetrator rapes: A national comparison of lone, duo, and 3+ perpetrator rapes. *Sexual Abuse, 26*(6), 503–522. https://doi.org/10.1177/1079063213497805

Decker, M. R., Wilcox, H. C., Holliday, C. V., & Webster, D. W. (2018). An integrated public health approach to interpersonal violence and suicide prevention and response. *Public Health Reports, 133*(Suppl. 1), 655–795. https://doi.org/10.1177/0033354918800019

Edmund, G., & Wortley, N. (2016). Interpreting image evidence: Facial mapping, police familiars and super-recognisers in England and Australia. *Journal of International and Comparative Law, 3*(2), 473–522.

Equality and Human Rights Commission. (2010). *Stop and think: A critical review of the use of stop and search powers in England and Wales*. https://www.equalityhumanrights.com/sites/default/files/ehrc_stop_and_search_report.pdf

Etgar, T., & Prager, K. G. (2009). Advantages of group therapy for adolescent participants in the same gang rape. *Journal of Child Sexual Abuse, 18*(3), 302–319. https://doi.org/10.1080/10538710902881329

Farrell, G. (2015). Preventing phone theft and robbery: The need for government action and international coordination. *Crime Science, 4*. https://doi.org/10.1186/s40163-014-0015-0

Farrington, D. P., Gill, M., Waples, S. J., & Argomaniz, J. (2007). The effects of closed-circuit television on crime: Meta-analysis of an English national quasi-experimental multi-site evaluation. *Journal of Experimental Criminology, 3*, 21–38.

Felson, M., & Clarke, R. V. (1998). *Opportunity makes the thief: A practical theory for crime prevention* (Police Research Series Paper 98). Home Office.

Gaffney, H., Farrington, D. P., & White, H. (2021). *Interventions to prevent school exclusion: Toolkit technical report*. Youth Endowment Fund. https://youthendowmentfund.org.uk/wp-content/uploads/2021/06/School-exclusions-technical-report-june.pdf

Gill, M., & Spriggs, A. (2005). *Assessing the impact of CCTV* (Home Office Research Study 292). Home Office. http://www.no-cctv.org.uk/caseagainst/docs/Assessing_the_impact_of_CCTV-HO_study292.pdf

Gov.uk. (2021). *Youth Crime Prevention Programmes*. https://www.gov.uk/youth-crime-prevention-programmes/

Guimarães, R. A., Mesquita, N. S., Lopes, R. S., Lucchese, R., de Felipe, R. L., Vera, I., Fernandes, I. L., de Castro, P. A., Monteiro, L. H. B., & Silva, G. C. (2017). Prevalence and factors associated with criminal behavior among illicit drug users: A cross-sectional study. *Substance Abuse & Misuse, 52*, 1393–1399. https://doi.org/10.1080/10826084.2017.1284231

Hadfield, E., Sleath, E., Brown, S., & Holdsworth, E. (2021). A systematic review into the effectiveness of Integrated Offender Management. *Criminology & Criminal Justice, 21*(5), 650–668. https://doi.org/10.1177/1748895820912299

Hare, R. D., Clark, D., Grann, M., & Thornton, D. (2000). Psychopathy and the predictive validity of the PCL-R: An international perspective. *Behavioural Sciences and the Law, 18*, 623–645.

Henderson, Z., Bruce, V., & Burton, A. M. (2001). Matching the faces of robbers captured on video. *Applied Cognitive Psychology, 15*, 445–464. https://doi.org/10.1002/acp.718

Her Majesty's Inspectorate of Probation. (2020). *The risk-need-responsivity model*. https://www.justiceinspectorates.gov.uk/hmiprobation/research/the-evidence-base-probation/models-and-principles/the-rnr-model/

Her Majesty's Inspectorate of Probation. (2021). *Integrated Offender Management*. https://www.justiceinspectorates.gov.uk/hmiprobation/research/the-evidence-base-probation/specific-types-of-delivery/integrated-offender-management/

HM Government (2020). *Neighbourhood Crime Integrated Offender Strategy: A unified approach to offender supervision in the community*. https://assets.publishing.service.gov.uk/government/uploads/system/uploads/attachment_data/file/942145/neighbourhood-crime-iom-strategy.pdf

HM Inspectorate of Probation and HM Inspectorate of Constabulary and Fire & Rescue Service. (2020). *A joint thematic inspection of Integrated Offender Management*. https://www.justiceinspectorates.gov.uk/cjji/wp-content/uploads/sites/2/2020/02/A-joint-thematic-inspection-of-Integrated-Offender-Management-2.pdf

Hodgson, B. (2007). Co-offending in UK police recorded crime data. *The Police Journal*, *80*(4), 333–353. https://doi.org/10.1350/pojo.2007.80.4.333

Hollin, C. R., & Palmer, E. J. (2009). Cognitive skills programmes for offenders. *Psychology, Crime and Law*, *15*, 147–164. https://doi.org/10.1080/10683160802190871

Hollin, C. R., & Palmer, E. J. (2020). The treatment and rehabilitation of property crime offenders. In A. Burrell & M. Tonkin (Eds.), *Property crime: Criminological and psychological perspectives* (pp. 221–233). Routledge.

Home Office. (2003). *Tackling personal robbery: Lessons learnt from the police and community partnerships*. Home Office.

Home Office. (2014). *Revised code of practice for the exercise by: Police Officers of Statutory Powers of stop and search. Police officers and staff of requirements to record public encounters. Police and Criminal Evidence Act 1984 (PACE)—Code A*. https://assets.publishing.service.gov.uk/government/uploads/system/uploads/attachment_data/file/384122/PaceCodeAWeb.pdf

Home Office. (n.d.). *Preventing youth violence and gang involvement: Practical Advice for schools and colleges*. https://assets.publishing.service.gov.uk/government/uploads/system/uploads/attachment_data/file/418131/Preventing_youth_violence_and_gang_involvement_v3_March2015.pdf

Home Office and Ministry of Justice. (2015). *Integrated Offender Management: Key principles*. https://assets.publishing.service.gov.uk/government/uploads/system/uploads/attachment_data/file/406865/HO_IOM_Key_Principles_document_Final.pdf

Hutchinson, J. (2020). Detective perspectives. In A. Burrell & M. Tonkin (Eds.), *Property crime: Criminological and psychological perspectives* (pp. 151–165). Routledge.

Jones, B., & Tilley, N. (2004). *The impact of high-visibility patrols on personal robbery* (Research Findings No. 201). Home Office.

Kitteringham, G. & Fennelly, L.J. (2020). Environmental crime control. In L.J.Fennelly (Ed.). *Handbook of loss prevention and crime prevention* (6th ed. pp. 207–222). Butterworth-Heinemann.

Lentz, S. A., & Chaires, R. H. (2007). The invention of Peel's principles: A study of policing 'textbook' history. *Journal of Criminal Justice*, *35*(1), 69–79. https://doi.org/10.1016/j.jcrimjus.2006.11.016

Local Government Association. (2020). *Taking a public health approach to tackling serious violent crime: Case studies*. https://www.local.gov.uk/sites/default/files/documents/10.46%20Taking%20a%20public%20health%20approach%20-%20Violent%20crime_03_0.pdf

MacDonald, J., Fagan, J., & Geller, A. (2016). The effects of local police surges on crime and arrests in New York City. *PLoS ONE*, *11*, 1–13. https://doi.org/10.1371/journal.pone.0157223

Machin, S., & Marie, O. (2011). Crime and police resources: The Street Crime Initiative. *Journal of the European Economic Association, 9*(4), 678–701.

Matthews, R. (2002). *Armed Robbery*. Routledge.

Mawby, R. C., Crawley, P., & Wright, A. (2007). Beyond 'polibation' and towards 'prisi-polibation'? Joint agency offender management in the context of the Street Crime Initiative. *International Journal of Police Science & Management, 9*(2), 122–134.

McCandless, R., Feist, A., Allen, J., & Morgan, N. (2016). *Do initiatives involving substantial increases in stop and search reduce crime? Assessing the impact of Operation BLUNT2*. https://assets.publishing.service.gov.uk/government/uploads/system/uploads/attachment_data/file/508661/stop-search-operation-blunt-2.pdf

McCardie, J., Storer, I., Torrens, G., Whitehead, S., Mailley, J., & Farrell, G. (2011). Offending users: Designing-in deterrence with mobile telephones. *The Design Journal, 14*(3), 323–342. https://doi.org/10.2752/175630611X13046972590088

Ministry of Justice. (2020). *Proven reoffending statistics quarterly bulletin, England and Wales, January 2018 to March 2018*. https://assets.publishing.service.gov.uk/government/uploads/system/uploads/attachment_data/file/872390/bulletin_Jan_to_Mar_2018.pdf

Ministry of Justice and Her Majesty's Prison and Probation Service. (2021). *Prison Population Figures 2021: Population Bulletin Monthly September 2021*. Dataset. https://www.gov.uk/government/statistics/prison-population-figures-2021

Monk, K. M., Heinonen, J. A., & Eck, J. E. (2010). *Street robbery* (Problem-Oriented Guides for Police Problem-Specific Guides Series No. 59). https://cops.usdoj.gov/RIC/Publications/cops-p181-pub.pdf

Motiuk, L. L., & Porporino, F. J. (1991). *The prevalence, nature and severity of mental health problems among federal male inmates in Canadian penitentiaries, R-24*. Correctional Service Canada.

Ormiston, S. (2021, October 7). *Motorbike machete gang mow down cyclist at 40mph to steal his bike in Richmond Park*. https://www.mylondon.news/news/west-london-news/motorbike-machete-gang-mow-down-21797918

Pettigrew, T. F., & Tropp, L. R. (2011). *When groups meet: The dynamics of intergroup contact*. Psychology Press.

Piza, E. L., & O'Hara, B. A. (2014). Saturation foot-patrol in a high-violence area: A quasi-experimental evaluation. *Justice Quarterly, 31*(4), 693–718. https://doi.org/10.1080/07418825.2012.668923

Piza, E. L., Welsh, B. C., Farrington, D. P., & Thomas, A. L. (2019). CCTV surveillance for crime prevention: A 40-year systematic review with Meta-analysis. *Criminology & Public Policy, 18*(1), 135–159. https://doi.org/10.1111/1745-9133.12419

Police and Criminal Evidence Act (PACE). (1984). https://www.legislation.gov.uk/ukpga/1984/60/part/I

Prison Reform Trust. (2019). *Prison: The facts.* http://www.prisonreformtrust.org.uk/Portals/0/Documents/Bromley%20Briefings/Prison%20the%20facts%20Summer%202019.pdf

Public Health England. (2019). *A whole-system multi-agency approach to serious violence prevention: A resource for local system leaders in England.* https://assets.publishing.service.gov.uk/government/uploads/system/uploads/attachment_data/file/862794/multi-agency_approach_to_serious_violence_prevention.pdf

Rajkumar, A. S., & French, M. T. (1997). Drug use, crime costs, and economic benefits of treatment. *Journal of Quantitative Criminology, 13*(7), 291–323.

Renzetti, C. L. (2008). Theories of criminal behavior. In L. Kurtz (Ed.), *Encyclopedia of violence, peace, and conflict* (pp. 488–498). Academic Press.

Rice, M. E., Harris, G. T., & Cormier, C. A. (1992). An evaluation of a maximum security therapeutic community for psychopaths and other mentally disordered offenders. *Law and Human Behavior, 16,* 399–441.

Ring, t. (2016). Humans vs machines: The future of facial recognition. *Biometric Technology Today, 4,* 5–8. https://doi.org/10.1016/S0969-4765(16)30067-4

Robertson, D. J., Noyes, E., Dowsett, A. J., Jenkins, R., & Burton, A. M. (2016). Face recognition by Metropolitan Police Super-Recognisers. *PLoS ONE, 11*(2), e0150036. https://doi.org/10.1371/journal.pone.0150036

Ross, R. R., & Fabiano, E. A. (1985). *Reasoning and rehabilitation: Manual.* AIR Training Associates.

Sentencing Council. (2021). *Robbery—Street and less sophisticated commercial.* https://www.sentencingcouncil.org.uk/offences/crown-court/item/robbery-street-and-less-sophisticated-commercial/

Silverton, K. (2020, July). *How Scotland's public health approach to tackling violence is reaping rewards.* https://www.place2be.org.uk/about-us/news-and-blogs/2020/july/how-scotland-s-public-health-approach-to-tackling-violence-is-reaping-rewards/

Sondhi, A., O'Shea, J., & Williams, T. (2002). *Arrest referral: Emerging findings from the national monitoring and evaluation programme* (DPAS Briefing Paper 18). Home Office.

Stockdale, J. E., & Gresham, P. J. (1998). *Tackling street robbery: A comparative evaluation of Operation Eagle Eye* (Crime Detection and Prevention Series Paper 87). Police Research Group.

Stripe, N. (2021). *Crime in England and Wales: Year Ending December 2020.* https://www.ons.gov.uk/peoplepopulationandcommunity/crimeandjustice/bulletins/crimeinenglandandwales/yearendingdecember2020

Sturge, G. (2020). *UK prison population statistics* (Briefing Paper Number CBP-04334). House of Commons Library.

Sutton, M. (1998). *Handling stolen goods: A market reduction approach* (Home Office Research Study 178). Home Office.

Swanson, C., & Livingstone, K. (2020). Situational crime prevention and crime prevention through environmental design. In A. Burrell & M. Tonkin (Eds.), *Property crime: Criminological and psychological perspectives* (pp. 203–220). Routledge.

Tilley, N., Smith, J., Finer, S., Erol, R., Charles, C., & Dobby, J. (2004). *Problem solving street crime: Practical lessons from the Street Crime Initiative*. Home Office.

Tiratelli, M., Quinton, P., & Bradford, B. (2018). Does stop and search deter crime? Evidence from ten years of London-wide data. *British Journal of Criminology, 58*, 1212–1231. https://doi.org/10.1093/bjc/azx085

Tong, L. S. J., & Farrington, D. P. (2006). How effective is the "Reasoning and Rehabilitation" programme in reducing reoffending? A meta-analysis of evaluations in four countries. *Psychology, Crime & Law, 12*(1), 3–24. https://doi.org/10.1080/10683160512331316

Travers, R., Mann, R., & Hollin, C. (2015). *Who benefits from cognitive skills training? Analytical summary 2015*. https://assets.publishing.service.gov.uk/government/uploads/system/uploads/attachment_data/file/448751/who-benefits-from-cognitive-skills.pdf

UNDOC. (2017). *Education and a tool to preventing crime and promoting a culture of lawfulness*. https://www.unodc.org/dohadeclaration/en/news/2017/02/education-as-a-tool-to-preventing-crime-and-promoting-a-culture-of-lawfulness.html

UK Government. (2021a). *Police powers to stop and search: Your rights*. https://www.gov.uk/police-powers-to-stop-and-search-your-rights

UK Government. (2021b). *Ethnicity facts and figures: Stop and search*. https://www.ethnicity-facts-figures.service.gov.uk/crime-justice-and-the-law/policing/stop-and-search/latest

UK Parliament. (2007, June). *Nature and extent of young Black People's over-representation*. https://publications.parliament.uk/pa/cm200607/cmselect/cmhaff/181/18105.htm

van Mastrigt, S. B., & Farrington, D. P. (2009). Co-offending, age, gender, and crime type: The implications for criminal justice policy. *British Journal of Criminology, 46*(4), 552–573. https://doi.org/10.1093/bjc/azp021

Waddell, S. (2020). *The role of primary schools in early intervention to prevent youth violence: Insights from work in two London boroughs*. Early Intervention Foundation. https://www.eif.org.uk/files/pdf/primary-schools-early-intervention-youth-violence.pdf

Wang, J., Paskevicius, A., Martinez nimi, H., Chacon, J. C., Ono, K., & Watanbe, M. (2020). Interaction modalities of personal security device design. *Journal of Security Design, 4*(2), 95–102.

Weine, S., Eisenman, D. P., Kinsler, J., Glik, D. C., & Polutnik, C. (2017). Addressing violent extremism as public health policy and practice. *Behavioral Sciences of Terrorism and Political Aggression, 9*(3), 208–221. https://doi.org/10.1080/19434472.2016.119841

Wellsmith, M., & Burrell, A. (2005). The influence of purchase price and ownership levels on theft targets: The example of domestic burglary. *British Journal of Criminology, 45*, 741–764. https://doi.org/10.1093/bjc/azi003

Wilson, S., Attrill, G., & Nugent, F. (2003). Effective interventions for acquisitive offenders: An investigation of cognitive skills programmes. *Legal and Criminological Psychology, 8*, 83–101.

Wolf, A., Gray, R., & Fazel, S. (2014). Violence as a public health problem: An ecological study of 169 countries. *Social Science and Medicine, 104*(100), 220–227. https://doi.org/10.1016/j.socscimed.2013.12.006

Wooditch, A. (2021). The benefits of patrol officers using unallocated time for everyday crime prevention. *Journal of Quantitative Criminology*. Advanced online access. https://doi.org/10.1007/s10940-021-09527-4

Wüllenweber, S., & Burrell, A. (2020). Offence characteristics: A comparison of lone, duo, and 3+ perpetrator robbery offences. *Psychology, Crime, and Law*. https://doi.org/10.1080/1068316X.2020.1780589

CHAPTER 8

# Conclusion

**Abstract** This concluding chapter brings together the key aspects from the book. A summary of chapters will be provided. This chapter will also include recommendations for future research to provide examples of how we can enhance our understanding of and ability to successfully detect and prosecute robbery in future. This will serve as a guide to students and applied researchers who are considering engaging in research that attempts to address this important (but often-ignored) offence.

**Keywords** Robbery · Future research · Key messages

## INTRODUCTION

The aim of this book was to draw together existing knowledge on personal robbery in the UK from across academic disciplines (e.g. psychology, criminology). This chapter summarises the content of the book and works to draw together key messages from the book.

Chapter 1 explained how robbery represents a tipping point between theft and violence, with the threats and force used being central to separating this offence from other theft offences. The focus on personal robbery in a UK context was emphasised though, from reading this book, it will be clear other perspectives are included where UK-focused examples

© The Author(s), under exclusive license to Springer Nature Switzerland AG 2022
A. Burrell, *Robbery*,
https://doi.org/10.1007/978-3-030-93173-5_8

were not available or difficult to expand. Definitions of robbery, trends in offending, and the impact on victims and society were also outlined. Chapter 2 focused on offender demographics and the motivation for offending. Personal robbery was identified as a predominately male-on-male crime committed against and by young males. Although money is a key motivation in robbery, other reasons including excitement and revenge also emerged. Key theoretical explanations for robbery offending were outlined. Chapter 3 focused on offence behaviour (e.g. target selection, weapon use) and methods (e.g. approach) used in robbery. There is also a discussion of offender adaptation and the potential implications of this (e.g. displacement). Chapter 4 moves the discussion onto group dynamics. Robbery is a predominately group offence and so the influence of people on each other is a key component of this offence, so much so that some offenders claim they only offend due to the undue influence of others. The impact of the group context on how offences are committed, such as level of violence, was outlined along with the potential impact of gangs and leadership on group offending.

Chapters 5 and 6 focus on behavioural investigative techniques, namely behavioural crime linkage (BCL), predictive profiling, and geographical profiling. A comprehensive discussion of the findings relating to BCL with personal robbery offences from the authors' PhD is provided. This guides the reader through what BCL is and how it might apply to personal robbery. Indications are that the theoretical assumptions of the technique are supported, but there are challenges presented by issues such as offender adaption and group offending. With regard to profiling, specific examples of testing or using these techniques with personal robbery were difficult to source. However, an explanation of the relevant theoretical frameworks and the evidence bases for these is included. There is also some discussion of typologies for robbery which acts as a foundation for future work in this area.

Chapter 7 provides a summary of the policing and prevention work that has been carried out to try and tackle personal robbery. These range from early intervention (e.g. education, mentoring) to policing approaches and offender treatment and rehabilitation. Multi-faceted, multi-agency approaches emerge as the most promising way to reduce robbery. This can provide layers of security and has the advantage of trying to intervene at lots of different stages of the offending journey. However, it is clear ongoing, robust evaluation will be needed to identify "what works" for reducing robbery.

## Key Messages

There are a number of key themes which emerge across different sections of the book. For the author, the key messages to take away are:

1. Personal robbery is worth researching!—this is a highly impactful crime and will re-remerge as problematic as new opportunities to commit it arise. Also, despite some really excellent work being done in the area, overall, there is a lack of in-depth, ongoing research. It is imperative to continue to research this area.
2. Try to stay ahead of technology—as technology advances, so do opportunities to commit crime and to prevent it.
3. Be aware of preconceptions and stereotypes—there are often preconceptions of what robbery is and who commits it. This can be borne out in data samples which might be skewed if particular people (e.g. ethnic minority groups) are disproportionately arrested and charged for robbery offences. It is important to remember that robbery is dynamic, nuanced, and committed by lots of different types of people for lots of reasons.
4. Problem solving and analysis is key—central to all crime prevention efforts is high-quality data, intelligence, and analysis.
5. We need to build the evidence base—there are lots of existing strategies that can be used/implemented to try to reduce robbery, but these are not always robustly evaluated and so knowing "what works" and why can be difficult to unpick. Work to explore what works and why is, therefore, an important avenue for future research.

## Future Research

Readers will have likely identified a range of areas where additional research on robbery would be beneficial. Particular areas that would be useful to (further) explore include:

1. Identifying characteristics of robbery—e.g. in different kinds of locations (to support the development of tailor-made tactics for prevention and intervention), trends over time, emerging issues (e.g. to predict new tactics robbers might use, who they might target, or what they might steal);

2. Interviews with offenders—including those who have not been incarcerated—about how and why they commit robbery to help inform crime prevention methods and boost desistence;
3. Research on how group dynamics impact on the nature of personal robbery—understanding how the group impacts on whether and how the offence occurs would support the development of educational programmes which focus on tackling peer influence;
4. Tests of how investigative methods—such as profiling and behavioural crime linkage—might work for personal robbery;
5. What works with robbery—for example, robust evaluations of tactics and interventions of strategies and interventions would be useful to build the evidence base around what works for reducing robbery and/or diverting people away from this type of offending. Evaluations should include consideration not just of what works but why—i.e. identifying the mechanisms for change. It is imperative to understand *why* interventions work—for example, if a mentoring scheme is effective, is this the programme? The staff? The location where it is delivered? A mix of different elements? etc. This is essential to understand if programmes are to be successfully replicated elsewhere; and
6. Research on the impact of new technologies on robbery—for example, are new opportunities created for offenders to commit crime? Are new opportunities created for prevention?

## Conclusion

There has been some high-quality research done on personal robbery (many of which are cited in this book) and it is hoped the book demonstrates the value of drawing from multiple disciplines when collating evidence about crime. However, it is noted that personal (or street) robbery remains relatively under-researched in the UK (Harding et al., 2019). Thus, the key, overarching recommendation from this book is that more attention is paid to robbery by researchers.

In terms of policing and prevention, there is no room for complacency. Robbery is a persistent problem and ongoing efforts are needed to keep crime rates down. New and emerging trends and technologies need to be considered. Existing frameworks can help to proactively identify emerging risks (e.g. using CRAVED to identify what the next "hot products" will be) and formulate solutions (e.g. using a situational crime prevention approach). For example, recent moves to increase the tap and PIN limit on debit cards to £100 (in the UK in 2021) will undoubtedly increase the value of stealing cards (Farrell & Tilley, 2021a, 2021b). This opportunity will not be missed by robbery offenders and safeguards will need to be put in place to minimise the impact when debit cards are stolen (e.g. limited number of tap purchases per day). A problem-solving approach is advocated with an emphasis on analysing the nature of the problem and using this to inform the development of tailor-made responses. Multi-faceted, multi-agency approaches are needed with developments in the public health approach offering good opportunities to reduce robbery.

## REFERENCES

Farrell, G. & Tilley, N. (2021a). Contactless card payment limits and crime rates after the pandemic. *UCL JDI Special Series on COVID-10: No. 26.* https://www.ucl.ac.uk/jill-dando-institute/sites/jill-dando-institute/files/26_contactless_payments_final.pdf

Farrell, G. & Tilley, N. (2021b). "Tap-and-PIN": Preventing crime and criminal careers from increased contactless payments. *UCL JDI Special Series on COVID-10: No. 28.* https://www.ucl.ac.uk/jill-dando-institute/sites/jill_dando_institute/files/tap_and_pin_no_28.pdf

Harding, S., Deuchar, R., Densley, J., & McLean, R. (2019). A typology of street robbery and gang organization: Insights from qualitative research in Scotland. *British Journal of Criminology, 59,* 879–897.

# Index

**A**
addiction, 25
Adolescent Limited Offender (AL), 28
anonymity, 27, 55
Area Under the Curve, 72

**B**
Bandits, 101, 104
Bayesian, 72
behavioural coherence, 62, 71, 103
behavioural consistency, 70–72, 80, 87, 88, 99
behavioural distinctiveness, 70, 99
Behavioural Investigative Advisors, 98
blitz, 10, 41, 100
British Crime Survey, 8, 22
buffer zone, 107
business robbery, 4, 5

**C**
Cambridge Harm Index, 11
carjacking, 45, 61
CCTV, 122, 127

Cognitive Skills Programmes, 130
co-offenders, 23, 37, 53, 55–57, 61, 62
co-offending, 6, 52, 55, 131
counting rules, 4
COVID-19, 27
Cowboys, 101, 104
CRAVED, 44, 122, 144
crime linkage, xi, 44, 46, 70, 71, 84, 85, 91, 97, 99, 142, 144
Crime Pattern Theory, 106
crime series, 46, 70, 99
Crime Severity scores, 13
Crime Survey for England and Wales, 6, 25, 37
criminal peers, 29, 63, 102
custody, 12, 13, 128, 129

**D**
definition, 1–5
de-individuation, 55, 60
Developmental Taxonomy, 28, 29, 31
diffused responsibility, 54
Discriminant Function Analysis, 72

© The Editor(s) (if applicable) and The Author(s), under exclusive license to Springer Nature Switzerland AG 2022
A. Burrell, *Robbery*,
https://doi.org/10.1007/978-3-030-93173-5

displacement, 45, 142
distance decay, 97, 107–110
diversionary activities, 119, 126
domocentricity, 97, 107
drug dealers, 5, 39, 63, 102
drug treatment, 126, 131, 132
duos, 59, 61

**E**
educational programmes, 118, 144
ethnicity, 22, 38, 55, 104
ethnic minority groups, 38, 125, 143

**F**
Facial recognition, 127
Financial loss, 9
firearms, 5, 43

**G**
gangs, 23, 53, 56, 63, 102, 142
geographical profiling, 97, 105, 108, 142
geography, 55, 82, 105, 108
group dynamics, 6, 44, 52, 59, 62, 64, 71, 103, 105, 119, 131, 142, 144
group offending, xi, 30, 53, 57, 59–63, 69, 85, 89, 91, 131, 142
group size, 55, 60, 61
group stability, 56

**H**
homology, 97, 99, 104
hot products, 44, 144

**I**
Impact on victims, 9
injuries, 4, 5, 9, 58, 60

Integrated Offender Management, 128
inter-crime distance, 70, 72, 74, 77–79, 82, 84, 88, 89
Iterative Classification Trees, 72

**J**
Jaccard's coefficient, 72
journey-to-crime, 104, 109

**K**
knife, 42, 43, 117

**L**
leadership, 62, 142
Least Effort Principle, 106
Life Course Persistent Offender (LCP), 28
linkage status, 72, 78, 79
Logistic regression, 78

**M**
Market Reduction Approach, 123
Ministry of Justice, 13, 14, 22, 117, 128
Money, 25, 31
mugging, 3
Multi Correspondence Analysis, 72

**N**
night-time economy, 6–8, 27

**O**
Offender adaptation, 45, 46
Office for National Statistics, 5, 7, 9, 13, 27, 38, 74
organised crime groups, 23, 25, 63, 102

## P
party lifestyle, 25, 29, 31
patrolling, 123
Peel, Robert, 118
peer influence, 26, 64, 144
3+ perpetrator groups, 59
physical violence, 54, 58, 61, 100
Police and Criminal Evidence Act (PACE) 1984, 23, 124
Principal Component Analysis, 72
profiling, 97–101, 103–105, 107, 108, 110, 111, 142, 144
Prolific offenders, 8
public health approach, 132, 145

## R
Rational Choice Theory, 106, 119
Receiver Operating Characteristic, 69, 72
reconviction, 118, 128
recorded crime data, 2, 74
Repeat victimisation, 8
Risk, Needs, Responsivity, 129
Robin's men, 101, 104
Routine Activity Theory, 105, 119

## S
Situational Crime Prevention, 118, 120
Social Control, 29, 31
Social Dynamics, 30, 31
Social Identity Theory, 52
Social Learning Theory, 29, 31
stop and search, 123–125
street crime, 3, 126
Street Crime Initiative, 117, 123, 126
street culture, 29, 102
street gangs, 23, 26, 55, 63, 102
street robbers, 38, 63, 124, 131
street robbery, 26, 27, 40, 63, 102, 110, 122, 124, 125, 127, 131
Substance misuse, 25
super-recognisers, 127
suspect prioritisation, 72, 99, 105

## T
tap-and-PIN, 45, 145
Target Selection, 37, 57
technological advances, 27, 45
temporal proximity, 70, 72, 74, 79, 80, 82, 84, 88
Theft Act, 1968, 3–5
Transport hubs, 8
trust, 30, 55
typologies, 99–104, 142

## V
victim resistance, 57
Violence Reduction Units, 132

## W
weapons, 30, 43, 44, 58, 88, 104, 125